D0596317

Contentment, Prosperity, and God's Glory

SERIES EDITORS
Joel R. Beeke & Jay T. Collier

Interest in the Puritans continues to grow, but many people find the reading of these giants of the faith a bit unnerving. This series seeks to overcome that barrier by presenting Puritan books that are convenient in size and unintimidating in length. Each book is carefully edited with modern readers in mind, smoothing out difficult language of a bygone era while retaining the meaning of the original authors. Books for the series are thoughtfully selected to provide some of the best counsel on important subjects that people continue to wrestle with today.

Contentment, Prosperity, and God's Glory

Jeremiah Burroughs

Edited by
Phillip L. Simpson

Reformation Heritage Books
Grand Rapids, Michigan

Contentment, Prosperity, and God's Glory
© 2013 by Reformation Heritage Books

Published by
Reformation Heritage Books
2965 Leonard St. NE
Grand Rapids, MI 49525
616-977-0889 / Fax: 616-285-3246
e-mail: orders@heritagebooks.org
website: www.heritagebooks.org

Printed in the United States of America
13 14 15 16 17 18/10 9 8 7 6 5 4 3 2

Originally published as "The Art of Improving a Full and Prosperous Condition, for the Glory of God," in *Four Useful Discourses* (London: Thomas Parkhurst, 1675).

Library of Congress Cataloging-in-Publication Data

Burroughs, Jeremiah, 1599-1646.
  [Art of Improving a Full and Prosperous Condition, for the Glory of God]
  Contentment, prosperity, and God's glory / Jeremiah Burroughs ; Edited by Phillip L. Simpson.
      pages cm. — (Puritan treasures for today)
  "Originally published as "The Art of Improving a Full and Prosperous Condition, for the Glory of God," in Four Useful Discourses (London: Thomas Parkhurst, 1675)."
    ISBN 978-1-60178-232-8 (pbk. : alk. paper) 1. Contentment—Religious aspects—Christianity. I. Simpson, Phillip L. II. Title.
  BV4647.C7 B78 2013
  248.4'859—dc23
                                                    2013009276

For additional Reformed literature, request a free book list from Reformation Heritage Books at the above address.

Table of Contents

Preface

Most of us would not consider ourselves wealthy. We compare our lifestyles to those of celebrities or famous CEOs, and the conclusion seems obvious: most of us are not rich, not poor, but right in the middle. We live average lives, earn an average income, and live within modest means in our average-size homes.

However, the words of the Puritan preacher Jeremiah Burroughs still hold true today: "We live here in such a way that, although we may not be as full now as we have been in the past, it may still be said of us that we are full in comparison to our brothers in other parts of the world."[1] Comparatively speaking, most of us really are wealthy to some degree. We live in comfortably heated and air-conditioned homes. We are amply supplied with well-made clothes. Most of us did not have to scrimp and save to purchase this book, but bought it

---

1. Jeremiah Burroughs, *Four Useful Discourses* (London: Thomas Parkhurst, 1675), 2.

when we first felt the impulse to do so. We may not like to admit it, but we are wealthy.

We might also wrongly assume that our wealth will never tempt us to be discontent. After all, why should we be discontent when we are well-supplied with nearly everything we want? However, it was the apostle Paul who said, "I have learned, in whatsoever state I am, therewith to be content. I know both how to be abased, and I know how to abound: every where and in all things I am instructed both to be full and to be hungry, both to abound and to suffer need" (Phil. 4:11–12). In other words, contentment is a lesson to be learned not only in times of hunger and want but also in times of fullness and abundance.

Burroughs, like Paul, experienced both times of need and times of abundance. He insightfully observed that the lesson of finding contentment in a prosperous condition was more difficult than learning contentment while in need. "You think it's hard for poor people to know how to be in want," he once said, "but the truth is, it's rather the harder of the two to know how to be full."[2] Because he personally labored to find contentment through such circumstances, it will be worth our time to give attention to Burroughs's insights on this matter.

Burroughs was born in East Anglia, England, in 1599.[3] After completing his master of arts at

2. Burroughs, *Four Useful Discourses*, 5.
3. The biographical information from this preface is condensed from *A Life of Gospel Peace: The Biography of Jeremiah*

Emmanuel College, Cambridge, in 1625, he was forced to leave Cambridge because he refused to conform to the unbiblical rituals, ceremonies, and superstitions the Church of England had begun to impose. However, this did not prevent him from entering the ministry. After serving two years as an assistant minister (curate) at All Saints Church, Stisted, he was appointed lecturer at Bury St. Edmunds in 1627. Lecturers were allowed to preach in churches where no suitable gospel preaching was available. Since lecturers were not formally licensed as ministers (vicars) of the Church of England, they were free from the restrictions placed on vicars. Burroughs served as lecturer in the same town as Edmund Calamy (1600–1666) and even shared a town lectureship with him. Burroughs's future certainly seemed bright. His heart's desire was to serve the Lord and His kingdom in as great a capacity as He would allow.

However, his lectureship at Bury St. Edmunds did not turn out as he had hoped. In 1630 he reported, "I have been nearly three and a half years with them with little success."[4] To make matters worse, the congregation seemed determined to get rid of him because he spoke

---

Burroughs, by Phillip Simpson (Grand Rapids: Reformation Heritage Books, 2011).

4. Jeremiah Burroughs to John Cotton, in *The Correspondence of John Cotton*, transcribed by Sargent Bush, ed. (Chapel Hill: University of North Carolina Press, 2001), 152–56.

out against a public sin committed by a local official. When the town voted to leave his pay at the discretion of his co-lecturer Henry White, he was left without any certainty of income. He was therefore forced to leave Bury St. Edmunds, taking a job offered to him at St. Margaret's in Tivetshall, Norfolk. This was somewhat disappointing to him; St. Margaret's was a small country church, and he felt that his ministry might be less effective than at the larger town of Bury.

Nevertheless, in 1631 he became the vicar of Tivetshall and served faithfully there for several years. He was even able to engage in rotating lectureships with William Bridge (1600–1671) and William Greenhill (1591–1671). However, when William Laud (1573–1645) was appointed archbishop, all ministers in England were required to read *The King's Book of Sports* from their pulpits. The *Book of Sports* was an official declaration of recreational activities in which the king's subjects were required to participate each Sunday. Such sports included "leaping, vaulting… May-games, Whitsun-ales, and Morris-dances, and the setting up of May-poles." For Burroughs and other Puritan ministers, this requirement violated their convictions regarding the sanctity of the Sabbath. Laud then appointed Bishop Matthew Wren (1585–1667) to visit the churches in Norfolk and report any nonconformists to him. Wren was especially zealous and enforced his own recently published "visitation articles," which contained 139 articles with 897 questions to be asked of ministers at these visitations. These included the following:

+ Does he receive the sacrament kneeling himself, and administer to none but such as kneel?

+ Does he wear the surplice while he is reading prayers and administering the sacrament?

+ Does he in Rogation-days use the perambulation around the parish?

+ Has your minister read the *Book of Sports* in his church or chapel?

+ Does he use conceived (rather than written) prayers before or after the sermon?

+ Are the graves dug east and west, and the bodies buried with their heads at the west?

+ Do they kneel at confession, stand up at the creed, and bow at the glorious name of Jesus?[5]

Burroughs could not in good conscience conform to such superstitions. His personal conviction was as follows: "In God's worship, there must be nothing tendered up to God but what He has commanded. Whatsoever

---

5. Abridged from *The History of the Puritans*, by Daniel Neal (London: William Baynes and Son, 1822), 2:247–48.

we meddle with in the worship of God must be what we have a warrant for out of the Word of God."[6]

When Wren's chancellor showed up at Tivetshall, Burroughs refused to conform and was subsequently suspended from the ministry in 1636. In 1637, his license was revoked, leaving him not only without a ministry but also without income. Fortunately, the Earl of Warwick provided shelter for Burroughs, as he had for many other Puritan ministers who had been similarly removed from public ministry. Earlier, Burroughs had expressed his hope of serving the Lord in a way that would allow him to do much good for His kingdom. Instead, his only preaching opportunities became those sermons preached before the Earl of Warwick's family and friends in the Earl's home.

To make matters worse, another minister accused Burroughs of justifying the Scots in their taking up arms against the king. Though the minister later recanted, officials continued with proceedings to arrest Burroughs. In late 1638, he fled England. Boarding a ship bound for Rotterdam, Holland, he accepted William Bridge's call to assist him as teacher there. This was an especially difficult time for Burroughs; he left behind many friends and earthly goods. Further, he was a patriot who loved England. "We scarcely thought we

---

6. Jeremiah Burroughs, *Gospel Worship* (Orlando: Soli Deo Gloria Publications, 1990), 10.

should ever have seen our country again," he said.[7] However, his sermons during this time never express a hint of complaint.

Burroughs's perseverance during this downward spiral of narrowing influence and ministry opportunities is exemplary. One reason for this was his view of contentment. Burroughs matched his own definition of contentment, possessing that "sweet, inward, quiet gracious frame of spirit" that freely submitted to and delighted in "God's wise and fatherly disposal in every condition."[8] For Burroughs, a Christian could find contentment in any circumstance if Christ Himself was his cherished possession. He said, "A Christian should be satisfied with what God has made the object of his faith (i.e., Christ). The object of his faith is high enough to satisfy his soul, were it capable of a thousand times more than it is. Now if you may have the object of your faith you have enough to content your soul."[9] While he was in Holland, Burroughs told his congregation that it was important to possess a "contentment of spirit that should be present in leaving all

---

7. Jeremiah Burroughs, *Sion's Joy. A Sermon Preached to the Honorable House of Commons Assembled in Parliament, at Their Publique Thanksgiving, September 7, 1641, for the Peace Concluded between England and Scotland* (London: T. P. and M. S., 1641), 41.

8. Jeremiah Burroughs, *The Rare Jewel of Christian Contentment* (Edinburgh: Banner of Truth Trust, 1964), 19.

9. Burroughs, *Rare Jewel*, 150.

for the cause of God."[10] By God's grace, he was able to do just that.

His contentment during these extenuating circumstances paid off, for in 1641 the new Parliament allowed all ejected ministers, including Burroughs, to return to England. Almost immediately he was appointed as lecturer to three large churches; two of these, Stepney and Cripplegate, were accounted to be England's largest congregations.

While he was at Stepney, Burroughs preached a sermon series that would later become one of his most well-received books: *The Rare Jewel of Christian Contentment*. This series of sermons was preached from Philippians 4:11–12: "I have learned, in whatsoever state I am, therewith to be content. I know both how to be abased, and I know how to abound: every where and in all things I am instructed both to be full and to be hungry, both to abound and to suffer need."

However, most modern readers of Burroughs are unaware that he followed this series on contentment in times of need with three sermons on achieving contentment during times of abundance. These sermons were compiled as an appendix to *The Rare Jewel of Christian Contentment* and were later published in the book *Four Useful Discourses*. This appendix was titled "The Art

---

10. Jeremiah Burroughs, *The Excellency of Holy Courage in Evil Times* (London: Peter Cole and Edward Cole, 1662), 65.

of Improving a Full and Prosperous Condition for the Glory of God." This lesson was especially needed for the congregation at Stepney, among which were many wealthy merchants and others of elevated social stature.

However, this lesson was not helpful for Burroughs's congregation only; Burroughs applied it to his own heart as well. His appointment to these large, wealthy congregations led to a new trial, one he called "the burden that is in a prosperous condition."[11] Being well paid for these lectureships (though he never sought a large salary), he was forced to find contentment in his newfound prosperity.

On the surface, this may seem like an easy venture; it almost seems unnecessary to instruct someone to be content in times of prosperity. However, Burroughs knew that he needed to learn to view this situation biblically. The truth is that times of prosperity and abundance can provide some of the strongest temptations to pull our hearts away from God. Those with wealth are often concerned with gaining even more, rather than living contentedly, as if their wealth contributed nothing to their happiness. It is often difficult for someone in a prosperous condition to truly live as if Christ is enough.

From all accounts, Burroughs seems to have won this inward fight for contentment in prosperity. He said of this struggle, "Through God's mercy, though I

---

11. Burroughs, *Rare Jewel*, 103.

have many weaknesses, and I fail in all that I do, yet I can say, to the praise of God, that my estate has not estranged my heart from God; rather, my heart cleaves to God, and I have communion with God in the things that God sends me."[12] His closest friends, including William Bridge, Thomas Goodwin (1600–1680), and William Greenhill, agreed. They noted how Burroughs labored to gain insight into biblical contentment and observed that he "has hewn forth this 'jewel'…out of the Rock, and has artificially cut it, that the innate rays of this, so glorious a grace, might shine forth to others."[13] Impressed with how his life reinforced his teaching on contentment, his friends remarked in their introduction to *A Treatise of Earthly-Mindedness*, "So, now, reader, you have these sermons twice printed: once in the practice of this holy man and once again in these papers which we present to you."[14]

Besides achieving popularity as a preacher, Burroughs was also given the honor of serving in the Westminster Assembly of Divines. He worked on the catechism and confession of faith and attempted—unsuccessfully—

---

12. Burroughs, *Four Useful Discourses*, 47.

13. Thomas Goodwin et al., "To the Reader," in *The Rare Jewel of Christian Contentment*, by Jeremiah Burroughs (London: W. Bentley, 1651), n.p.

14. Thomas Goodwin et al., "To the Reader," in *A Treatise of Earthly-Mindedness*, by Jeremiah Burroughs (Morgan, Pa.: Soli Deo Gloria Publications, 1998), iii.

to obtain toleration for those convinced of a congregational form of church government. In addition, he was given the honor of preaching before Parliament on several occasions.

Burroughs was not without further trials during this phase of his life. He likely did not marry until he was in his early forties; the couple remained childless. One of his most difficult trials took place when he became the target of vitriolic attacks by men like Thomas Edwards (1599–1647) and John Vicars (1582–1652), who sought to undermine Burroughs's ministry by writing slanderous treatises against him. These attacks burdened Burroughs's spirit so much that his health suffered. Despite all this, his character remained so exemplary that his fellow Puritan ministers marveled at his ability to maintain a peaceable, godly spirit.

Burroughs died in 1646 following a fall from a horse. He had become so beloved in London during these years that, following his death, it was reported that he was "a man much lamented."

The book you now hold contains Burroughs's original appendix to *The Rare Jewel of Christian Contentment.* It is presented here to the modern reader with editorial changes to improve readability. In addition, Burroughs preached a sermon to Parliament on the same subject.[15]

---

15. Jeremiah Burroughs, *A Sermon Preached before the Right Honorable House of Peers, in the Abbey at Westminster, the 26th of*

Although Burroughs used the same text (Philippians 4:12), and many of the points overlapped, he included new material not found in the sermons he preached at Stepney. Therefore, some of the material from his parliamentary sermon has also been assimilated into this present volume, since many of these points and illustrations are helpful and applicable to the modern reader.

It is my prayer that Burroughs's words will grip your hearts, as they have continued to grip mine. Like Paul, and like Burroughs, we need to learn contentment in prosperity as well as in need. May we use all that we have been given in such a way as to bring our God the greatest glory.

Phillip L. Simpson

November, 1645, Being the Day Appointed for Solemn and Public Humiliation (London: R. Dawlman, 1646).

CHAPTER 1

Introduction

I know both how to be abased, and I know how to abound: every where and in all things I am instructed both to be full and to be hungry, both to abound and to suffer need.

—Philippians 4:12

It is a common saying that there are many people who are neither well when they are full nor when they are fasting. If they are in affliction, then they are obstinate and discontented. If they are in a state of prosperity, they are unruly. Just like children, they cry and are obstinate if you do not let them have what they want, but if you do let them have what they want, then they are unruly. They cannot behave orderly either way. There are some people who are of such irritable and unpleasant dispositions that no matter what condition they are put into, they are obnoxious. There are some who have unpleasant hearts, and they are unpleasant in every circumstance they encounter. But Paul, by the work of the grace of God, was fitted for all circumstances—not only for affliction, but if God willed that he be prosperous, then he could tell how to make use of that. "I know both how to be abased, and I know how to abound: every where and in all things I am instructed both to be full and to be hungry, both to abound and to suffer need" (Phil. 4:12). But what were the specific circumstances that led Paul to make these statements?

Context of the Passage

Besides the apostolic call Paul had to preach to all nations, he had a special, extraordinary call to preach to these Philippians: "And a vision appeared to Paul in the night; there stood a man of Macedonia, and prayed him, saying, Come over into Macedonia, and help us" (Acts 16:9). Philippi was the first place in Macedonia where he preached; it was a chief city in that part of Macedonia (16:12). But was Paul encouraged by the fruit of this extraordinary call? One would have thought that the people would have immediately come to embrace the gospel, that the hearts of the people would have been mightily stirred. But Paul's preaching was, at first, not so successful. The first Sabbath that he went there, he went to a riverside to preach.

Did the nobles, the magistrates, the gentry, or the chief citizens come out to hear him? No, only a few women came out to hear him, for verse 13 says, "We sat down, and spake unto the women which resorted thither." Did the Word of God have any effect on any of the women? Yes, for it says that "a certain woman named Lydia, a seller of purple, of the city of Thyatira, which worshipped God, heard us: whose heart the Lord opened" (16:14). Though he had no better success at first, it was possible that his preaching might prove more successful afterward.

The next thing we hear of Paul is that he, along with Silas, was dragged rudely before the magistrates by the multitude, accused of troubling the city. The magistrates viewed Paul and Silas as vile men, guilty of horrible things, and became enraged against them. They tore their clothes and whipped them; they put them into prison, where they were thrust into the dungeon and put into stocks. Was this the fruit of Paul's wonderful call of God, his vision from heaven? And was it such fruit as this that encouraged a man of such a mighty apostolic spirit as Paul to come to Philippi to preach?

Oh, what sad and discouraging circumstances some men encounter in the work that God has called them to! Learn by this never to conclude that a work is not of God just because you encounter discouraging circumstances at first. Pour your hearts out to God and rest in His call; good fruit will come about in the end.

The spirits of Paul and Silas were not disheartened by this lack of success, for in 1 Thessalonians 2:2 Paul tells us that "even after that we had suffered before, and were shamefully entreated, as ye know, at Philippi, we were bold in our God." There was finally a church in Philippi that was as free from contamination and as eminent in godliness as any. Though men may scheme, condemn, and cast dirt upon a certain movement—even stirring up the authorities and the people against it—still, it may prevail at last.

In Philippians 1:3–4, Paul says, "I thank my God upon every remembrance of you, always in every prayer of mine for you all making request with joy." Though these Philippians were moved at first, did the work of the gospel on their hearts endure? Many seem to be effectively changed by the gospel when they first hear it, and their situation looks hopeful, but after a while this all vanishes and comes to nothing. But this was not the case with the Philippians, for in verse 5 he says that their fellowship in the gospel had continued "from the first day until now," which had been about ten years. Many churches, when they first gather, have sweet fellowship, but in less than five years it is interrupted by divisions, and its former glory becomes darkened.

At this time Paul was in prison at Rome. The Philippians, who had heard the gospel through Paul's ministry, sent Epaphroditus to minister to Paul when they heard of his imprisonment. They also sent gifts by Epaphroditus to give relief to Paul and to provide for his necessities. It is worth noting that Paul's sufferings did not cause them to lose their affection for Paul or his doctrine. If someone wants to prevail against the people of God, against Christian truths, or against the ways of God, they should not use violence against them to do so; hypocrites may be prevailed against that way, but those who are sound in the faith will be strengthened even more solidly by such means.

Now, when the Philippians sent supplies to relieve Paul in prison, he took the occasion to write this epistle to them. In the epistle he rejoices at their care for him. However, he was aware that someone might have accused him of merely loving them in order to receive gifts from them; indeed, such gifts can often become snares to ministers of the gospel. Therefore he responds by saying, "No, it is not because I am lacking anything that I am writing this epistle to you. I am not bothered by being in need, so don't think that I desire to profit from my imprisonment. 'I have learned, in whatsoever state I am, therewith to be content.' Let me be in need or not; it makes no real difference to me, for 'I know both how to be abased, and I know how to abound...in all things I am instructed.'"

Notice how Paul says, "I know." Humility is a *knowing* grace. By this, Paul does not mean he knows how to abase and abuse himself; that would be foolish. Neither is he saying that he knows how to suffer, because when God calls him to suffer he will suffer; that would be silliness. Rather, when Paul says, "I know...how to be abased," he means that he has learned to *submit* to suffering in a humble manner. Humility can be borne of fear or of ignorance or of lack of skill, but the humility of which Paul speaks here is a knowing humility.

Also, when Paul says, "I know," he means "I *have* known it; I have been acquainted with this. I am not about to begin learning it now. When God first called me, He showed me what things I must suffer for His name; it is not a lesson to learn now. I know how to be abased, for I have learned it in Christ's school; I have even learned how to be trampled under the feet of others." A godly heart is willing to lie under the feet of anyone for the sake of good.

Finally, when Paul says, "I know how," he means that he knows how to rightly judge his abasement. He knows not to look at it as a repulsive thing, as carnal hearts would, but to see honor in his abasement. If I know how to be abased, then that means I know how to interpret God's intention for my abasement differently than the world does. I know how to bear it with a quiet spirit; I know how to satisfy my heart in the midst of it. I know how to improve my abasement for the glory of God and for the spiritual good of my own soul, as well as that of others. I know how to exercise faith and other graces in the midst of it. I know how to get the sting out of it; I know how to remove the venom from it. I know how to carry myself in a gracious, comfortable, and heavenly manner in the midst of my abasement. Although the world may put dishonor upon me, I shall not dishonor myself or my cause by any unseemly behavior. It appears that Paul did indeed know how to do this, for his gracious character while he was chained in bonds actually helped to further the conversion of many, including some from Caesar's court (see Phil. 4:22).

Introduction to the Topic

In another book, *The Rare Jewel of Christian Contentment*, I discussed the doctrine of the Christian's contentment in any circumstance. In the closing portion of that book I propounded several considerations for Christian contentment. I then gave several directions regarding what we are to do in order to exercise the grace of Christian contentment.

Among all others, there is one special thing that I commended and would still point out, and that is that you make a good interpretation of God's mercies and dealings toward you. Have good thoughts of God and make good interpretations of His dealings toward you. It is very hard to live comfortably and cheerfully among friends when one makes harsh interpretations of the words and actions of another. The only way to keep sweet contentment and comfort in Christian societies is to make the best interpretations of things we can. Likewise, a primary way to help to keep comfort and contentment in our hearts is to make good interpretations of God's dealings with us.

I will leave it to God to bless those lessons that have already been delivered to you, and I hope that when any temptation arises for discontentment, some of the truths you have received may come to mind. I also hope that when some of you see others discontented (such as a wife with her husband, a husband with his wife, or one brother or friend to another), you may be able to use something from this text to counsel them regarding this grace of contentment. Although I spent a long time teaching this lesson, yet it is a longer lesson to learn than it is to teach. You will need a longer time to learn it than I have spent teaching it. We will not learn it in a few weeks; we will need to spend years learning this great lesson.

Now we come to another lesson that is just as hard to learn: namely, how to be full. "I am instructed," says Paul, "how to be content in all states; I am instructed how to be full. If God sends in supplies to me, if He gives me respect and honor among the churches, I know who to look up to as the cause of it all. I know how to carry myself in a holy and spiritual manner in the midst of all these enjoyments. If God gives me so much that it runs over, I know how to make good use of it."

Now this is a hard lesson, but because these are times in which people generally suffer and don't have as great abundance as they formerly enjoyed, I had intended not to expand upon this argument as much as I had upon the other. That seemed to be more suitable. However, the truth is that we live here in such a way that, although we may not be as full now as we have been in the past, it may still be said of us that we are full in comparison to our brothers in other parts of the world. Besides, perhaps God will hasten our fullness if we are taught how to be full before fullness comes. I will now open up this lesson—"I am instructed how to be full," says the apostle—any conditions, either full or empty, either way.

There is a parallel passage to this in 2 Corinthians 6:8. Paul describes the different conditions that he went through "by honour and dishonour, by evil report and good report." Sometimes the apostles had honor, sometimes they had dishonor; sometimes people spoke well of them, and sometimes they spoke ill of them. "Yet," he says, "we went through it all; we carried on the work of the gospel in all things." So, in verse 10 he says, "As sorrowful, yet always rejoicing; as poor, yet making many rich." "Whatever our condition was," he says, "yet through the grace of God we were carried through it all, and we did so in a manner so as to sanctify God's name and to further the gospel in it." Many men are prepared for one condition, but they are not prepared for another. This, by contrast, was the excellence of the grace of God in the apostle: he was prepared for any condition that God might turn him toward.

The Doctrine Presented

Now then, regarding this lesson of being full, this is our primary point:

A Christian is taught by God to know how to be full.

The Christian learns this lesson. There are many who would gladly hear a lesson on how they could obtain fullness, but they do not consider it as necessary to learn how to sanctify God's name in their fullness. If I could preach a sermon or two to you on how you could supply your wants and how to obtain wealth, I have no question that our church would be filled with people. This would be the case if we were to teach poor people how they could get rich, to teach those who are disgraced how they could get honor, to teach men how they could have good and prosperous journeys, and the like. But I am teaching you a lesson from God rather than man at this time, and that is much better. It is a better lesson for one to learn how to honor God in fullness than it is to learn how he can get full.

It is a good sign that truth and grace are working in your heart if you judge this to be the better thing. That is, it's better to know how to honor God with those good things I have than to know how I can get more. It's better to know how I might behave myself in the enjoyment of those good things God has given me than to know how to get more of those good things. God has given me a reasonably large estate, in that my house has fullness in it, and I have everything I need. It may be you do not have as many fine things as others have, but what do many of you lack in your houses? You have all kinds of household items that are necessary for you and a convenient diet that is also necessary for you. You are therefore full because you have all things that are necessary, even though you may not have everything on which you have set your eye.

We used to say that it's better to fill a child's belly than his eye. Perhaps your every whim is not supplied, but your necessity is supplied. When the necessity of a person is supplied, his condition is said to be full. Therefore, let not those who are in a poorer condition than others think this lesson does not concern them. While it is true that you do not have as much as others have, you do have enough to keep you in health and strength, fit for God's service. Besides, I am sure that you all abound more than Paul, and yet he said, "I have all, and abound, and am full." Oh, that you would apply your hearts to learn how to abound in what you have. It's a good sign of grace to be more concerned about how to abound than how to get abundance—to be more careful to use what you have for God than to maintain it for yourselves.

Therefore, since this argument is of great necessity and use (as I hope shall be obvious before I am done), I shall unfold this lesson, dividing it into the following headings:

+ When may a man be said to have learned how to be full? "I am instructed," says Paul, "and know how to be full."

+ How difficult it is for us to learn how to be full

+ What a great need there is for us to learn how to be full

+ What an excellent thing it is for a man to know how to be full

+ What mystery of godliness is found in knowing how to be full

+ What the several lessons are that Christ teaches the soul in order to learn how to be full

+ What conditions aggravate the contemptibility and guilt of sins related to abundance

+ The application of it all

CHAPTER 2

What Learning to
Be Full Means

What do I mean when I say that Christ teaches His people to know how to be full? When has a man learned how to be full? There are several evidences that indicate when a man has learned how to be full.

1. A man has learned to be full when he has learned to set a suitable price on his fullness. When he has learned to set a due price and value upon those mercies God has been pleased to grant to him, when he can prize such mercies—not too highly, nor too lowly, but as they are—he has learned how to be full. No man can attain to the grace of Christian contentment if he is unable to handle his affliction; he must understand and know his affliction, or he cannot come to Christian contentment. Similarly, we cannot learn how to be full unless we understand the mercies God has granted to us. If a man should enjoy many mercies and does not understand them, he has not learned how to be full. He must prize the mercy God has granted to him at a suitable rate.

As he considers even these outward mercies as the good blessing of God toward him, he must not slight them; he must look upon them as coming to him from the promise: "Godliness is profitable unto all things, having promise of the life that now is, and of that which is to come" (1 Tim. 4:8). It is a fruit of the promise of God to him. God's goodness is meant to encourage him in the way his righteous God has set him in. He must consider the outward blessings he enjoys in this way. In other words, he must regard these things as good utensils (if I may call them that) that allow him the opportunity to do service to God in the place where God has set him.

This, then, is how we are to estimate their true value: realize that they give greater opportunities for the service of God than those who are in a more meager condition have. A poor man may be as precious to God as you, but it may be that he can do little for Him because he does not have the ability to use outward things the way you do. You enjoy many blessings, but what is so great about that? Rather, you ought to say, "I praise God for these outward blessings, but what causes me to praise God most are the opportunities these things give me to honor His name—opportunities I would not have otherwise." Can you honestly, before God's presence, say this?

Many great men judge the value of their honors and estates by the increased ability and opportunity such things give them to satisfy their lusts. They count themselves fortunate that they may do so with no self-control and in ways that others cannot afford. However, a godly man must prize good things according to their true value. You should estimate the value of your estates and honors by the opportunities they provide for service. A man who slights God's mercies and thinks there is little value in them does not know how to be full.

But now, just as he must not prize them at too low a rate (that is, his health, his estate, and the comforts he has), neither should he prize them at too high a rate. They are mercies, but they are only outward mercies. It's true that such material things are good blessings from God—but they are common blessings. Though a Christian is able to recognize the source of every mercy in a way that the ungodly person cannot, yet God's goodness in general is enough to bestow the things themselves.

Indeed, I have them, but they are nothing more than a reprobate may have as well. They are good things, but they are not so good that they make anyone become good. Though we may say, "Such a man is the most prominent man in the church," yet certainly his things do not make him any better; only grace can do that. These things that he has may be good, but they may not be good for him.

There are good things, however, that are not only given by God freely but that *are* acceptable to Him. That's the difference between all the good things of which we now speak (such as fullness of estate and the outward comforts of the world) and the things of grace. The things of grace are given by God freely, and they help those people who receive them become better in God's eyes. But now, let God give ever so many outward things, they will never make a man one whit better in God's eyes.

An ornate, calligraphic letter in a word adds no more meaning to the word than any other letter; neither does the enjoyment of fancy material things make a man the better for it. These things are no more signs of a good condition than a face painted with makeup is a sign of true beauty! You would be a fool to choose a wife based on how well she applies makeup; it would be foolish to judge her beauty according to her makeup. Certainly it makes as much sense to argue for her beauty based on her outward cosmetics as it does to argue that riches and honors prove someone's worth in God's eyes.

Yes, these things are blessings, but they are blessings on the one hand only; they are only outward blessings. If these things are truly good things, it is only because your good character guides you to use them for good. Just as a man's clothes are first warmed by the heat of his body before they provide warmth for him, a man's happiness is not derived from having these things, nor is his misery a consequence of lacking them. They make no great difference to a man's condition. Therefore, a man must learn to rightly value his fullness. That's the first thing.

2. A man learns how to be full when he can discern the best use of what he has—that is, when he can tell how best to distribute the fullness God gives him. When a man can tell how much he really needs for himself, when to make use of any given human comforts, and how little or how much use to make of them—then he has learned how to be full. There are many men who do not know how to use their fullness. First, they do not know how to prize it; they do not know the true worth of it. Second, they do not know how to make use of what they should, how much or how little, or at what time they should make use of the good things God gives them. And so they come to be excessive, even defective, in the enjoyment of what the Lord has given them.

Some are excessive in this; even though they have an abundance of human comforts, they still take in more than is in any way useful to them for their fullness. They justify their excesses by saying, "I may do whatever I want with what I own." It is not enough to say that just because a man's drink is his own, therefore he ought to drink as much as he pleases; or, because his meat is his own, therefore he should eat as much as he will and to not know how to order himself and be moderate; or, because his estate is his own, therefore he should spend it as he likes in an excessive way.

A philosopher once reproved a man who had feasted excessively. Someone asked him, "Why do you reprove him? He spends nothing but that which belongs to him." The philosopher answered him, "Is this a good answer—that you are spending only what belongs to you? Suppose your cook has a great deal of salt, and he put two or three handfuls of it into your meat to season it. And suppose that when asked why he did so, he answered, 'I had enough salt, and the salt did not cost much; I had plenty in the place where I store it,' or, 'I can purchase more salt at a better rate.' Would this be a good answer?" So it is not enough for us to say that our estates are our own, and therefore we may be excessive in our use of our possessions. No, you have not learned how to be full until you have learned how much you really need for your own use.

Perhaps God has given so many great things because He intends for you to use them for something other than yourself. God gives you so much a year, but not because He intends for you to spend it all to fill your own belly or to clothe your own back. You have not learned how to be full until you have learned how to properly distribute the use of your estate and outward comforts that you enjoy, according to the needs that exist.

A man learns this lesson when he makes no more use of what he has than is appropriate for him, even though he is in the midst of abundance. Though a man is at a feast where there are a great many dishes, is it enough for him to say, "It was a happy, festive occasion" in order for him to justify his gluttony? But a man shows he knows how to be temperate when he is in the midst of a great many dishes and knows which are most fit for his body and feeds moderately on them. That's the second thing. The first is how to put a due valuation upon mercies, and the second is how to apportion the use of mercies, using only so much at such a time and so much at another time.

3. *A man learns how to be full when he can use the comforts he has received but does so in a way that avoids the evil of the temptations that go along with them.* As we shall see later, there are many temptations that go along with fullness. A man who learns how to be full uses his possessions but is still able to deliver himself from the evil of the temptations that accompany his fullness. It takes a wise man or woman to know how to do this—to be able to distinguish between the good and the evil of the temptation that goes along with any good thing.

Many times you consume whatever you can get but without any consideration of what temptation may go along with it. You think there is no temptation in the fullness that you have. However, you are wiser with yourself in other ways. No one says, "Whatever comes into a fish net must be all fish; therefore, let's eat all of it." Or, let's say you eat a fish that is full of little bones. You will pick out those little bones rather than swallow it whole. So you should consider when God gives you fullness that there may be many little bones together with it. Yes, and if you're not careful, they may be wrapped up in such a skin as will be bitter to you, unless you remove them first. If you swallow the fish down whole, it may even be poisonous. Now, men and women know how to be full when they can tell how to pick out the temptation of it; they are able to enjoy the thing while avoiding its temptations.

There are some, because they hear there are many temptations in the enjoyment of their comforts, who think there is no other choice but to fling such comforts away. One man, after seeing many who had been hurt by their wealth, cast his money into the sea, saying, "I will drown you before you drown me!" But this is not what it means to learn how to be full, to say, "Because I must avoid the temptation, I must not enjoy the comfort of the blessing." Many men and women, through weakness and tenderness of conscience, are afraid that they will get hurt by using the things God has given them. They therefore deny themselves much of the comfort they would have in those things. While God may accept their desires to honor Him and their fearfulness of sinning against Him, choosing such a course of action nevertheless is a sign they possess a great deal of weakness.

The strength of a Christian is to enjoy God's gifts, to make use of whatever God allows, to take the sweetness from it, and yet to avoid the temptation—in other words, to take away that which is good and to cast away that which is not good. There are many kinds of meats, but you ought not to eat all of them. A child often thinks he or she must either have it all or nothing. That is why you would not give the child good meat that has something bad mingled with it, because the child does not know how to pick out the bad and eat only the good. But someone who has understanding knows how to pick out the good and fling away that which is not good, and yet not to fling it all away just because there's something in it that is not good as well as good.

"The prosperity of fools shall destroy them," said Solomon (Prov. 1:32). The foolish hear of men who are so taken with the sweetness of their prosperity that they scarcely give any serious thought to the dangers in it so that they may avoid it. Now that's the third thing, and there are very few who understand this lesson; they must swallow down everything without first considering the temptations that may be attached to the fullness they enjoy.

4. *A man knows how to be full when he can keep under his command everything he enjoys, and he can retain command over his own spirit in what he enjoys.* Therefore, he is not a slave to what he has, but he makes what he has a slave to himself. You say of some rich men that they have certain possessions; the truth is that their possessions have them rather than they have their possessions. Their possessions rule over them.

A man knows how to be full when he makes all that he has to be his underling, his servant. He makes it serviceable to himself, and he can command anything that he has, according to its usefulness. He will never be a servant to his servant. It's a sordid disposition for any man to be a servant to his servants, but many of you have become a servant to your estates. They command you, and you (as well as your honor) have become a servant to them. This is a sign that you don't know how to be full. A man doesn't know how to rule if he allows himself to be under his servant; likewise, a man does not know how to be full if he does not have command over what he enjoys in the world—or better yet, command over his own spirit in the use of what he enjoys.

To have command over one's spirit means that a person can let out as much of his heart to his possessions as is useful—and no more—and then is able to call his heart back in again when he needs it. Ordinarily, people do not let their spirits out to only a little joy, but they let them out to such an extent that they have no command over their spirits. They have lost their spirits; they cannot call their spirits back in again in order to be serious and humble and to be mourning for sin when God calls them to it.

Now, for instance, when you say you will be merry and go visit your friends and have good cheer, God allows you to do so, as long as you know how to make good use of it. But do you let out your hearts so far that you cannot call them back in again? Again, do you let your spirits out so far in mirth that when it's time for you to go and humble your souls before God in prayer, your hearts have become light and vain? Then you have no command over your spirits at all, and perhaps the next day you are worse for it. Your hearts are just like little children: let them have anything they wish for a little while, and you will find yourselves unable to rule over them for many days or weeks later. So when you let your hearts have liberty for a little while to rejoice in created things, you may find you have no command over your hearts for several weeks.

Now, being merry is certainly permissible; religion does not prevent you from times of mirth. But our mirth should be such that we have command over our spirits so that we can call our hearts back in again when there is occasion. I will rejoice in created things, yes, but I will reserve my primary joy for something else. There is something else that I am to rejoice in more than the use of such things. If you let out your heart in such a way that you rejoice in created things so as to make them your primary joy, your only joy, then such joy is not right. But it is not so with the heart of a man who knows how to be full.

5. *A man has learned how to be full when he can use the gifts of God and yet remain ready to part with all his comforts if God calls for them.* If I enjoy comforts, but in such a manner that my heart lies down before God and is prepared to give up those comforts I enjoy whenever

God would have me do so, then I have learned to be full. People may have hearts that cling so tightly to their possessions that they cannot leave them, no matter what comes of them. They must preserve their assets at all costs. Now that they have had wealth and have had whatever they needed supplied to them, they cannot live meagerly; they are willing to venture into sin or anything else in the world in order to preserve their estates. It's as if they say, "Oh how is it possible for a man who has had such an upbringing as I have had to be put into such straits that I can scarcely have bread?" And after considering this thought they will do anything they can to keep their wealth, whether God wills it or not. They will do this rather than allow themselves to part with their comforts when God would have them do so.

Oh, if you act in this way, you have not learned how to be full. If your heart were right, you would enjoy the comfort of your possessions when God gives them, but if God were to take them you would say, "Lord, if Thou hast use of them in any other way, here I am; do with me what Thou pleasest. The Lord gives, and the Lord takes away; blessed be the name of the Lord. I'll take them as long as Thou wilt have me do so, but when Thou art ready to sanctify Thy name in my poverty, Lord, take them from me." We are too passionate about created things when our hearts cleave to them, and taking them away rips our hearts.

Many men's spirits are like a bee: when it comes to sting, it thrusts its stinger so far in that it cannot be taken out, so the bee leaves it in there. Likewise, our hearts are so riveted into our possessions that we cannot part with them; when God is ready to take them away from us, they are so dear to us that they cannot be removed. That's the reason people cry out the way they do; that's why they complain that they are undone and wring their hands, even if they have lost only part of their estates and even if they still have a great part of it still remaining. Oh, how they will wring their hands as if they were undone! This, then, is a sign that they did not learn how to be full while they had their fullness.

A man has never learned how to be full if he becomes immoderately sorrowful when God takes away his possessions. This is what it means to know how to be full, when we can tell how to enjoy things as well as how to be without them. Oh, think of this when you are at your full tables: "Now I have all these things around me, but if God should call me to suffer poverty, could I then be content to lie in a prison for His name's sake?" Paul, when he was in his fullest condition, stood ready and able to take his heart off of it. He could say, "Oh, Lord, if Thou wilt honor Thyself by me—whether in a prison or by poverty or by disgrace—why, Lord, here I am." He was already prepared. You know that you have not learned to be full unless you can find yourself, in the midst of your fullness, ready and prepared to part with all your fullness for Jesus Christ.

By just naming these things I suppose you all think this is a hard lesson to learn. You may think it's hard for poor people to know how to be in want. While that is hard, the truth is rather that the harder of the two lessons is learning how to be full. That's the fifth thing in which a man may know if he has learned how to be full.

6. *A man knows how to be full when he can make all his fullness to further grow in all his graces—to act upon his graces, to exercise his graces, and to draw forth his graces.* For instance, he can make the fullness he has a means to grow in the grace of love—to love God in all his fullness (not so much to love the things themselves, but to love God in the things). It can also exercise his grace of heavenly-mindedness if he prays in this manner: "Oh, Lord, these comforts that Thou hast given me in Thy gifts, oh, they are sweet—but how much sweeter is Thyself! How sweet is Jesus Christ! That is the fullness of all this fullness! And if this life is so sweet here in this world, what dost Thou have then in the heavens to make me to long after heaven?"

Further, he can use his fullness as a means to help his faith. He can pray, "Lord, Thou hast said that godliness has the promise of this life and the life that is to come. Why, Lord, Thou hast made this promise good to me, and this strengthens my faith." A man's fullness can also exercise the grace of charity to others. A man has learned how to be full when he knows how to exercise his graces by his fullness. While fullness may deaden the graces of other men, fullness will strengthen the graces of someone who knows how to be full.

Such a man learns fullness when his grace stirs him up in thankfulness to God and when it encourages him in the duties that God requires of him. "Oh, I receive such wages" says a gracious heart; "I receive much from God. Surely, then, there must be much work required of me. I receive more than others do, and therefore it is fitting that I should do more work than others do." Thus, a Christian learns to be full when his fullness serves to further his graces.

7. A man knows how to be full when his fullness leads him to the source of his fullness—that is, when his grace leads him to God. When a man knows how to enjoy God in his abundance, to be led to Him by his possessions, to acknowledge Him in all things, and to be thankful to Him in all things, he has truly learned how to abound. It is not the created things themselves that satisfy such a man, but God in them. Created things are simply the channel that lets God into their hearts. Isaiah 6:3 says, "The whole earth is full of his glory." But it may be more properly translated, "His glory is the fullness of the earth."

A man who has truly learned how to abound will say, "It is the glory of God that completes and gives fullness to my estate, honor, and comforts. It is communion with God that I enjoy in these things, and that's what truly causes my soul to rejoice. It's true that the ordinances are the special channels God uses to communicate His goodness to me; nevertheless, I do experience the sweetness of His love, and I enjoy a certain communion with Him in these outward things, and that means more to me than the entire world."

In Philippians 4:7, the apostle Paul says that "the peace of God…shall keep your hearts." But in verse 9 he says, "The God of peace shall be with you." For someone with a grace-filled heart, it is not enough to have the peace of God; he must have the God of peace. It is not enough to have honor from God; he must have the God of that honor. All the riches in the world cannot satisfy him unless he has the God that gave him those riches. You have finally learned how to abound when your heart can pass quickly through created things and move on to enjoy God as your most prized possession. But where is the man who enjoys more of God in abundance than in want? A Christian, then, learns to be full when his fullness can carry him to God, who is the source of all his fullness.

8. A Christian learns to be full when he can spread out all his fullness and offer it to God for His use—that is, when he can improve what he has to serve God. I use it, yes, but I do not use it for myself so much as for God. I know how to be full when I can see the opportunities for service that God has given to me in my fullness. Hasn't God given me a larger opportunity for service than others? Well, then, let me improve it for the public good. Perhaps I have been raised to a position of public service. Others may not be able to be engaged in public work as I am because they are poor, even though they may be just as capable for such service with regard to their gifts and graces. Therefore, I will improve my fullness in my public work, that I may be a useful man in the place where God has set me. Let me be as full of good works as possible, so that I may be a public blessing to the place where the Lord has placed me. This attitude shows that a man has learned how to be full.

9. *A man learns to be full when he uses the things of this world as if he did not use them (1 Cor. 7:30–31).* A man does so when he enjoys the fullness of his outward things, but only as incidentals; that is, he enjoys them but does not depend on them for his joy. He has comfort in them, but his comfort does not depend on them. Most people enjoy their outward possessions in such a way that such things are their whole treasure. They do not use them as incidental things but as their *end*— not as a *means* to the end, but as their end. A man has learned to be full when he can use his fullness, not as his end but as a means to the end—not as things that he depends upon for his happiness but as things that are incidental.

Combine all these points, and it will describe for you the man who has truly learned what it means to be full. Therefore, Paul said, "I am instructed both to be full and to be hungry, both to abound and to suffer need." Oh, I urge you, even before you learn anything further: apply these particular lessons to your hearts. I appeal to your consciences today in the name of God: Have you learned how to be full? Many of you are full with regard to outward things, but have you been in Christ's school to learn to enjoy your fullness in this way?

I am truly persuaded that many of your consciences will cause you to have uneasy thoughts today about these things—that is, if you really do believe that these are the truths of God (and I cannot imagine any of you would not be convinced of this; therefore I do not need to develop this any further or provide Scripture proofs). Every man's conscience will tell him, "Certainly I have not learned these things; I have not learned to be full— that is, I have not learned to sanctify the name of God with my fullness."

Allow your conscience to reprove you for being truant in the school of Jesus Christ; let this humble your souls before the Lord. I will discuss this in more detail later, but for now know that this is your work: to go and be humbled before the Lord because you have not understood what it means to sanctify God in the fullness that you enjoy. Pray in this way: "Lord, through Thy mercy I have been full of outward comforts my whole life. In

Thy mercy Thou hast been so generous toward me. But Lord, though I have enjoyed fullness for a long time, oh, how far have I been from knowing how to be full. If this is what it means to know how to be full, then I have been a stranger to it up until now."

10. *A man knows how to abound if he knows how to make use of his worldly comforts, yet is able to do so in such a way that he is not hindered by the afflictions or troubles that go along with those comforts.* When men abound and are full of comforts in this world, they cannot avoid having some affliction and troubles that go along with these comforts. All creature comforts are mingled with troubles.

Now, then, a man rightly knows how to be full when he enjoys his fullness in this way: although he has some affliction mixed with it, he is able to use such affliction to humble himself; at the same time, he is also able to thank God for his comforts. Many people enjoy their comforts, but if they encounter any trouble or affliction that mixes with their comforts, they become so filled with anger and bitterness and their spirits become so troubled that they lose all the goodness they should have gotten from their comforts.

For example, Haman abounded, but he did not know how to abound. Therefore, when he became aggravated in one thing (that Mordecai did not bow the knee to him), why, all the comfort of his prosperity vanished. His spirit was filled with rage, bitterness, and malice.

And so it is with many people who have abundance in their families. They are full of outward comforts—they have their friends and children, they have estates, they have their tables well-furnished, and all the things that one would think would make the heart of almost any man content. But if a single aggravating circumstance arises that displeases them, they are thrown into such an angry and fretting condition that they lose all the benefit of their comforts.

Do you know how to abound? When you go out and encounter something that displeases you, do you immediately fly off into a rage and begin fretting and forget to thank God for all your mercies? Do you find nothing but fretting and aggravation in your family for one displeasing circumstance, when there are a hundred mercies for which you should bless God?

You do not know how to abound when you cannot take into account the good of mercy when you consider an affliction. Even when God afflicts you in something, He still gives you an abundance of occasions to bless Him and praise Him. But when you can bless God for all mercies and be humbled for all afflictions at the same time, then you are a man who knows how to abound. It's a sign that you have truly learned how to abound when you can say, "If God grants me more mercies than afflictions, He shall have more thanksgiving from me than sorrow"; or (regarding troubles), "I'll have more joy than I will have trouble"; or, "I have more mercy than I have correction."

11. Finally, a man has learned how to abound if he knows his own heart in the midst of his abundance. It's common for people not to know themselves once they come into abundance. Saul was little in his own eyes when he was in a meager condition, but when he came to abound he did not know himself. That's the way it has usually been with people: their abundance removes from them the very knowledge of themselves. They grow reckless and foolish and proud so that they no longer know themselves once they have abounded. But when a man in the midst of his abundance knows his own baseness, wretchedness, sinfulness, and vileness, regardless of his abundance, he is a man who has learned the apostle's lesson regarding how to abound.

I have given various reasons why the lesson of knowing how to be full is more difficult than knowing how to be empty. Surely learning how to abound is very difficult if it requires that we learn lessons like these. While few people in the world will agree, certainly this is the case.

Although just naming these things demonstrates how difficult a lesson it is, I want to go further and show you more specifically the tremendous difficulty there is for men and women in knowing how to be full. I mention this to you because I want you to pay attention, so that you may not pass over this lesson lightly. After all, men who have large estates and outward comforts are very prone to slighting the Word of God. If you'll indulge me, I would like to show you more regarding the difficulty of this lesson, that you may not slight it.

Sailors are not so concerned about maneuvering a ship if they are given enough room at sea to do so. They find this to be an easy part of their job; as long as they have enough room at sea, they feel safe doing so. But this is not the case when you have the great sea of prosperity. In a vast sea of prosperity you actually fare far worse for yourselves. It is the abundance of outward prosperity that is the undoing of most men. The more abundance you have, the more difficult it will be for you to know how to order yourselves as you go about your business. An abundance of pleasures is surely difficult to navigate safely; as one early church father said, no sins are more difficult to overcome than sins of pleasure. Extra space, extra freedom to maneuver around, may be your undoing.

To change the analogy slightly, it is much easier for someone to manage a little boat in the river than for one to do so with a large commercial ship. Likewise, less skill is necessary to order a man's estate when he is poor and lives meagerly in the world than when he attains a full condition. It would be madness to allow a man who can row only in the river to take command of one of our greatest ships. So it is for those who are poor: unless God teaches them how to be full, they are as likely to undo themselves by their fullness as by any other way. It is easier for a man to manage his small estate than for him to manage great commerce. It is likewise harder to manage fullness than being poor; more skill is required to manage fullness than is required otherwise.

It is like how extreme heat is harder to bear than cold; even when it is very cold, by exercise we may warm ourselves. But when the weather is extremely hot, that is very hard to tolerate, and it breeds diseases. It is also easier to carry a cup that is half full steadily than to carry a cup that has been filled to the brim.

Those who can demonstrate a great amount of grace in times of adversity will then in times of prosperity lose the graces they apparently had before; they simply let it all go. You know the fable of the sun and the wind, wagering which could get into the traveler's coat. When the wind came blustering and blowing, that could not do it, but the warm sun shed its beams, and the traveler immediately threw his coat off. A tempestuous storm will make a traveler pull his cloak closer together and hold it tighter, but when the warm beams of the sun come and shine upon him, he takes off his cloak. So also will the warmth of prosperity cause one to shed the graces he held tightly in times of adversity. Manna could endure the heat of the fire because the people baked it, but it melted under the heat of the sun. Many have been melted under the heat of prosperity, losing their godly character, though they previously withstood the scorching heat of affliction.

CHAPTER 3

The Difficulty of Learning to Be Full

As I stated in the last chapter, men think it's a hard thing when they are brought low under affliction, but in truth it is much harder to know how to abound. You who are well-to-do think that you are much better off than those who seem to live under the enemy's rage. You enjoy so much, and you are thankful. You must admit that, compared to them, you have been greatly blessed. You are under the impression that the lesson they are learning, that is, how to bear patiently while they remain under such great afflictions, is very hard. The truth is, however, that between the two of you, you have the harder lesson to learn. It is harder to know how to abound than to know how to be in want. This may seem like a paradox, but before we are done I hope to make this truth completely clear.

The Difficulty of Learning How to Abound

There are various reasons I will give you why this is such a difficult lesson to learn.

1. The first reason this is so difficult is because we are mostly flesh; there is more flesh than spirit in us. Because we have so little spirit in us, all the things that the flesh draws toward must be dangerous for us to manage. I am not speaking of our corruptions at this point, but of those natural things—things that pertain to our senses, which our flesh is drawn toward. All of us have lost, to a great extent, the image of God that we were meant to bear. The best of us have only a little of the image of God remaining in us, and some have lost it to an even greater extent. Further, our ability to reason has been wounded by our fall into sin.

Therefore, having so little strength in our spirits, we fall into great danger by those things that the flesh is drawn toward; they greatly weaken our better part. Adversity pulls the heart away from the flesh, takes it off the flesh, and many times makes the spirit stronger; but those things that add strength to the flesh endanger us. It is more dangerous to set a child upon a pampered horse than upon a horse that has been wearied out with work. So also we who are weak in our spirits will find that there's a great deal of danger in having our flesh pampered and fully satisfied. I am still speaking only of those things that pertain to our senses and our natural flesh.

2. In prosperity there are more duties required of us than in adversity. A poor man does not have that many duties required of him, but a man who enjoys a full condition has an abundance of duties required of him. Every comfort he enjoys carries with it an obligation to some special duty. A poor man works hard at his day's labor and has nothing else to do but bless God when he comes home to his family, to look to his own heart, and to serve God in his family. However, a man who is full, who has a large worldly estate, is required by God to look beyond his home to the general public. God gives him the charge, "See to it that My worship is set up. See to it that justice is executed. I will require these things at your hand. See to it that My Sabbaths are not profaned. See to it that godliness is accepted and that sin is frowned upon."

But perhaps you will say, "Every man who is rich is not a justice of the peace, or in a similar position." Yes, but by your visible position you will make friends with this person and that person; everyone is bound to be a friend to those who are rich. There are a great many duties that are required of you that are not required of the poor. If indeed a man who had a wealthy estate had nothing else to do but sit by the fireside and have his servants bring him provisions—if this was all that was needed to be full—it would be easy for a man to know how to be full. But you must know that there is much more that falls on your shoulders than this—things for which you must answer and for which you must give an account before God. This is what makes it so difficult.

3. *There are a variety of temptations that go along with a full condition.* Oh, there are an abundance of temptations in a full condition, much more than there are in a lowly condition. I admit that extreme poverty has many temptations with it, very sore and grievous temptations, but not as go along with a full condition. As sweet things such as honey attract an abundance of flies, so also does the sweetness of prosperity attract Beelzebub, whose name means "god of the flies." Oh, the devils that have that name will come in abundance whenever they see sweetness, whenever they see much prosperity. Rats and mice come to full barns, not to empty ones, and so the vermin of temptations, as I may call them, pay much attention to those in a full condition.

Suppose someone who is hungry passes by a tree with nothing on it. He will not sling anything at it since there is no fruit to be gained from it. However, he will sling something at a tree full of fruit. Likewise, the devil passes by those who are in a poor and low condition, but he especially labors at those whom he sees who have much of the world; he has higher hopes of gaining something from them.

It is very interesting to compare the two places in Scripture where the conditions of Joseph's blessing are given: the one is in Genesis, where Jacob blesses Joseph, and the other is in Deuteronomy, where Moses' blessing was given. In Deuteronomy 33:13–16 we read, "And of Joseph he said, Blessed of the LORD be his land, for the precious things of heaven, for the dew, and for the deep that coucheth beneath, and for the precious fruits brought forth by the sun, and for the precious things put forth by the moon, and for the chief things of the ancient mountains, and for the precious things of the lasting hills, and for the precious things of the earth and fulness thereof." As for all his outward blessings, Joseph had a great abundance of precious things; he was full of these blessings.

But notice this: Out of all the tribes, what is said of Joseph? Genesis 49:22 says, "Joseph is a fruitful bough, even a fruitful bough by a well; whose branches run over the wall." But now notice what is said in verse 23: "The archers have sorely grieved him, and shot at him, and hated him." None of the other tribes had been blessed with so many precious things as had Joseph, yet the archers shot at none of the other tribes as they are said to have shot at Joseph. Therefore, by comparing these two Scriptures, you see that those who have most of the precious things of this world are the most likely to be shot at; the devil shoots at them more than he does others.

Furthermore, just as there are a greater variety of temptations with a full condition, so also these temptations are better suited to the natural man. The devil can prevail more in his temptations with fullness than with want and emptiness. Why? Because although there are temptations in a poor condition, they are not so pleasing to a man's own nature as the temptations of a full condition. A poor man is tempted, but what is he tempted to? He is tempted to impatience, but that's not a pleasing thing. Rather, it's a tedious thing. He is also tempted to despair, but there's no pleasure in that either. He is tempted to take shifty courses of action, yes, but even in that there is a fear that he might be discovered, and so be punished.

The temptations of a poor man are not as well suited to his human nature when they are compared to the temptations of a wealthy man. The wealthy man's estate is a temptation to pride, to uncleanness, or to overindulgence. Such things are suitable to the very nature of a man. Therefore, there's a lot more danger in the temptations that go with fullness than by want because the temptations of poverty are tedious to a man's nature, but the temptations of wealth are suitable to a man's nature.

Suppose that you had a bitter-tasting poisonous plant in your house. It's true that it may do harm, but it's not as likely to do so as sweetened rat poison. That's because even though it has poison in it, yet it has a sweet flavor too. There is poison sometimes in a poor condition; that is, there are temptations to great evils in a poor condition. Yes, but those temptations have bitterness in them. By contrast, the temptations of a full condition have sweetness in them, and therefore there's a greater danger in them, making it more difficult to avoid those temptations.

Further, the temptations that come from fullness are subtler. Those that come from want are not as subtle; they are more obvious. But the temptations that go along with a full condition are, for the most part, in lawful things, and it is in these things that we most often fail. When the temptation comes along, it sounds so reasonable. We are tempted to say, "Why? May a man not take liberty to comfort himself in God's gifts? May a man not take what is his own? May not a man make use of what is his own?" For the most part, all the temptations of fullness, or a great part of them, appear in things that seem to have no harm in them; therefore, they are subtle, and a man needs to be very cautious of them. They are (as we have said before) like little bones in a fish that you can hardly see; there's a lot more danger in swallowing them down, compared to other prickly things. And so the temptations of a full condition come along very secretly; it's very hard to see them unless you look very closely.

4. *Fullness not only provides a temptation to sin but also provides fuel for all kinds of lusts.* Fullness will feed these lusts if you have not learned how to be full. For example, if a man struggles with the lust of pride, a full condition provides him with the ability to act on his pride; he will feed it to the full. Fullness will also make a proud man become a contemptuous man, so that he will scorn and jeer, not only at his brothers but at God, His truth, ministers, and religion—all because he is full. His pride has been fed to the full.

Fullness will also feed self-love to the extreme. When a man perceives himself to be self-sufficient, he sees no need for God or Christ or mercy or the Word and its promises. It will also feed his hatred. If he has a malicious spirit against another man, he has the power to undo him; he can spend whatever he has to in order to get his way. It further feeds his stubbornness. If he wants to be unclean, he can, for who will meddle with him? It will also feed his licentiousness. He is at liberty and rides up and down from place to place, doing whatever he pleases. A poor man might have just as much inclination to satisfy his lusts, but he must attend to his work, or his family will starve. Yes, but a man who is in a full condition has room enough to satisfy his lusts. He can go out in the morning and stay till midnight and do this from the beginning of the week to the end of it and still not be in want.

Oh, a prosperous condition is immensely pleasing to the flesh; it feeds a man's lusts and makes them stronger. This is the reason the Word rarely ever does any good to those who are full. Ordinarily, the poor receive the gospel; the Scriptures say, "Not many rich, not many mighty, not many great ones." Why? Because they have so many material goods with which to feed their lusts that their lusts grow too strong. These lusts become so strong that they resist the Word; they resist all means that might do them any good. Therefore, it's very hard for a man to learn how to be full. Yes, and it is for this very reason (that is, that fullness can give strength to lusts) that this is such a necessary lesson, though a hard lesson. What condition will a man be in, then, who is full and yet, for all that, has not learned to be full? If he has such provision for his lusts and does not know how to order himself, he is likely to be a lost man.

There is one more reason why it is so difficult to learn how to abound.

5. *A full condition is in danger of hindering those graces that are distinctly Christian.* If a prosperous man does not learn how to abound, these graces become exceedingly endangered. It is very difficult for men or women to carry themselves with any measure of stability when siege is being laid to those graces that are uniquely Christian.

For example, the graces of a Christian include faith, self-denial, humility, patience, tenderness, and others such as these. A prosperous state mightily endangers these graces. Consider the grace of faith. You know that the nature of faith is for someone to be emptied of himself and to see that there is nothing in and of himself. Rather, he is to rely upon another outside of himself. This is the grace of faith, then: to remove any grounds of reliance upon ourselves, or from created things, and instead to cast ourselves upon free grace, upon the goodness and mercy of God, and upon the righteousness of Another. A full state very much hinders this life of dependence, which is the life of a

Christian. Yes, the life of a Christian is even more of a life of dependence than was the life of Adam; therefore, a low condition is more suitable to a life of dependence than a full condition.

The same can be said of the grace of self-denial. It is easier for someone who is in a low condition to deny himself. But when a person comes into wealth, he grows accustomed to having himself pampered, as it were. For him to then deny himself and be nothing in his own eyes becomes a great deal harder.

And so it is with the grace of humility. It's not that much for someone who is poor and in a low condition to have his heart kept low, but for someone to have his heart low when his condition is high is much more difficult. Men's hearts naturally rise as their estates rise; as their comforts rise, so their hearts will rise. Therefore, when learning how to abound, the lesson of growing in the grace of humility is a very difficult lesson to learn.

And then there's the grace of tenderness—of a tender heart, a soft heart. That's a grace that belongs to a Christian in a special manner: to keep constantly tender and soft-spirited. Now, although the hearts of many become tender and soft in times of affliction, yet once they come to prosper their hearts become hard. The prosperity of the world "bakes" their hearts (as it were) and hardens them. As the sun hardens the clay, so prosperity hardens the hearts of men and takes away any tenderness that might have been. We all could readily call to mind, with no difficulty whatsoever, numerous examples in which this has been the case.

Evidences of the Difficulty in Learning to Abound

I would now like to give you further evidences that demonstrate the difficulty in learning to abound.

1. The first evidence is the solemn and frequent charges God gives to His people to take heed to themselves when they are full. In Scripture we never find God solemnly and frequently charging His people to watch themselves when they are in want to take heed *then* not to forsake Him. Though there are some commands that way, they are not given in such a solemn way as God does when He speaks to those who are likely to be in a full condition. To them God says, "Look to yourselves." For example, in Deuteronomy 6:11–12, God says that His people were to have "houses full of all good things, which thou filledst not, and wells digged, which thou diggedst not, vineyards and olive trees, which thou plantedst not." And then, "When thou shalt have eaten and be full," says the text, what then? "Then beware lest thou forget the LORD, which brought thee forth out of the land of Egypt, from the house of bondage."

The time when people are the least careful is when they eat and are full; then they think they are in no danger at all. Yes, but this is the charge of the Spirit of God: when you have eaten and are full, that's when you need to be especially careful. Remember this, you who have full tables! Oh, that this Scripture were written over your tables and were in your thoughts when you come to your full dishes, when you eat and drink and become full. It would be nothing more than a disheartening thought to some of you to think this way: "Oh, I must be even more careful than before."

Some of you have been in a poor state. Perhaps you were only a poor sailor on a ship at first, but after a few voyages you traded, invested, and raised up an estate. This, then, is a text that concerns you. Has God given you such voyages, that now your house is full? You used to have empty houses, but, as is common with sailors, you now have your houses full of good things that you bring from beyond the sea. Now, when your houses are full, says the text, beware that you do not forget the Lord; rather, at that time you should fear Him.

In Deuteronomy 8:10–14 you have this charge repeated by the Lord, not once, but twice. He says,

> When thou hast eaten and art full, then thou shalt bless the LORD thy God for the good land which he hath given thee. Beware that thou forget not the LORD thy God, in not keeping his commandments, and his judgments, and his statutes, which I command thee this day: lest when thou hast eaten and art full, and hast built goodly houses, and dwelt therein; and when thy herds and thy flocks multiply, and thy silver and thy gold is multiplied, and all that thou hast

is multiplied; then thine heart be lifted up, and
thou forget the LORD thy God.

See what charges are here; it's as if God should say, "I
am not so concerned about you while you are in the wil-
derness, while you are empty, but I am very concerned
about what you will do when you are full. I am afraid
that then you will forget Me."

Therefore you see how it is repeated again in Deuteronomy 11:15–16. He says, "And I will send grass in
thy fields for thy cattle, that thou mayest eat and be full.
Take heed to yourselves, that your heart be not deceived,
and ye turn aside, and serve other gods." Take heed,
then, that you do not become deceived when you are full.
There is a great deal of deceitfulness in riches, and the
Scriptures speak of this. You might say, "Why, when we
are full, we intend to eat and drink, and to enjoy the pleasure of what God has given us." Oh, but take heed that
you are not deceived. Since God gives such caution and
solemn charges to us again and again, in Deuteronomy
6, 8, and 11, surely He would have us learn that there is
a great deal of danger in being full. Therefore, it is a difficult lesson for us, to know how to be full and abound.

2. *Further evidence that this lesson is a difficult one to learn
lies in this question: When do you find throughout all the
Book of God that a full condition ever turned any soul to
God, or was the means of doing so, when that person had
not turned to God before?* I can find in Scripture that an

afflicted condition has been blessed by God, so that it has been an occasion to turn some to God. For example, it is reported in 2 Chronicles 33:6 that King Manasseh "wrought much evil in the sight of the LORD, to provoke him to anger." However, verse 12 says that "when he was in affliction, he besought the LORD His God, and humbled himself greatly before the God of his fathers." And so God often speaks once and twice, and men do not hear, but then He opens their ears by correction: "In their affliction they will seek me early" (Hosea 5:15). But do you ever find it to be the case that those who did not seek God before were drawn to God by a full condition? Truly I can find no examples of this in Scripture, where the prosperous estate of a man was the occasion leading to his conversion. Therefore, that shows that there is a great deal of danger in a fuller condition.

3. *Furthermore, how often do you find that any of God's children who were brought into a full condition became worse for it rather than better?* It's true that you may find a few examples where we read that they were not worse for their prosperity, such as Nehemiah and Daniel, but how often can you find an example besides these? Almost all others, once they became prosperous, forgot God. They would not benefit spiritually from their conditions until they were afflicted. David had learned to be content in his afflicted condition, and he benefited greatly from it. Oh, but he did not learn so well how to

be full. Therefore, you shall find that the most excellent psalms that David ever penned were when he was in his afflicted condition. There was a fullness of the Spirit of God in him then at that time in a more special manner. Therefore I remember that it's said in one place that Jehoshaphat did according to the first works of his father David (2 Chron. 17:3). The first works of David were the works he did when he was not so full, but when he grew to be full, his works were not so good then.

Generally, all the people of God have been worse in a full condition. So it is with Solomon. You know how his fullness nearly spoiled him. Even though he had so much wisdom that he understood almost all things, he lacked the wisdom to know how to be full. There was never a man of such greatness in the world (that was merely a man) who had the wisdom that Solomon had, and yet all his wisdom was not enough to teach him the lesson of knowing how to be full.

4. *God's use of affliction as a tool for sanctification is evidence of the difficulty in learning to abound.* The way of God has constantly been, even from the beginning of the world to this day, to keep His people down low in affliction, especially in the times of the gospel. This, then, is evidence that it's a very difficult thing to learn how to be full. Why is it that the Lord, in His providence, has so ordered things that most of His churches and His saints should be kept under affliction? He could just as easily

fill them full with outward blessings as He fills them with the Holy Spirit. Yet those whom God fills with the Holy Spirit He does not ordinarily fill with outward blessings; rather, the people of God have ordinarily been in affliction. This is an evidence to us that God sees that it is more safe for them to be in a lowly state than in a high one because they can better learn how to be empty than to be full; therefore, He rarely brings them into a full condition.

Daily experience teaches this too. Who are those who are the most spiritual and heavenly Christians? Are they those who are the fullest? We see plainly that it is otherwise. Oh, God has a great deal more glory from poor, lowly Christians; there is more spiritual communion between God and them than there is between God and those who are in a prosperous state.

There is a noteworthy story from church history that underscores this point. In the fourth century, after the church had been delivered from persecution, the emperor Constantine endowed it with great possessions. The story says that there was a voice heard in the air saying, "This day is poison poured into the church." And, as events unfolded, the church did indeed grow far worse after it was delivered from persecutions. It was in a worse condition by far than when it was under persecution. They could not learn to be full like they could learn to be afflicted and empty. They then fell into contending and wrangling with one another, and heresies began to prevail a great deal more than they did when they were under persecution.

We also find this to be so by our experience. Is it not so that when we are the lowest, then we are in the best condition for the most part? For as soon as we have prosperity and are full, we begin to kick and fuss. So this is the second point, that it is a very difficult lesson to learn how to be full.

CHAPTER 4

The Necessity of Learning to Be Full

Although learning how to glorify God in a prosperous condition is a very difficult lesson to learn, it is still a necessary lesson. There is a kind of absolute necessity of learning it, a great necessity. There are several reasons there is a need for this lesson, and it would be a sad thing if you did not learn it.

1. If those who are full do not learn how to be full, they will be guiltier of abusing the gifts of God than other men. The things God has given them, which they enjoy more abundantly than others, will be in bondage, so to speak, and will cry out against them. Let me ask you: Do you not enjoy many more things than those who are in a poor condition? But if you have not learned how to use them for God, night and day these things from God will cry out to heaven against you. It's as if these things are saying, "Lord, we were made for Thee, and we have the ability within us to be useful for Thy glory. But the person Thou hast allowed to possess us abuses us and

forces us away from the purpose for which Thou hast
made us, the purpose for which we would have gladly
been useful. Lord, we are being forced to do what is
contrary to our nature; we were never made to be serviceable to the lusts of men. Yet this man abuses us
according to his lusts. Lord, why should we be in bondage to a man like this, who abuses us in this way?" You
would not like being a servant to someone who abuses
you. Likewise, the things God has created groan, as
it were, under the bondage they are in when men and
women enjoy them in their fullness and yet abuse them;
they groan when they are not working toward the end
for which God made them. There are cries that God
hears from the things He has created, though you do
not hear their voices.

2. *If you are in a prosperous condition and have not
learned how to be full, then you will be guilty of sinning
against God's mercy more than others.* God has been
merciful in bestowing many things upon you. If you use
such mercies only to add to your own sinfulness, this
becomes a grievous condition. Mercy is a tender thing;
therefore, sinning against mercy is a very grievous thing.
Those who are in a low condition have many mercies,
but not as many as you; therefore, they are not guilty of
sinning against mercy as much as you are. What a sad
thing this is—that God's mercy, which ought to do us
much good, should be used by us for nothing else than

to add to our sins. There's nothing that more aggravates our sin than sinning against mercy.

Therefore, when the Lord speaks to the very heart of His people to persuade them, He reminds them to consider His mercy toward them. Deuteronomy 32:6 says, "Do ye thus requite the LORD, O foolish people and unwise?" So, do you thus repay the Lord? Has God made your condition more comfortable than others'? Another man needs bread, barely gets by, must sleep on a hard surface, is in the cold, and lives in a poor condition; you are fully supplied with everything you need around you, and yet are the worse for it? Is this how you repay the Lord, oh foolish heart?

You know that this was what added to the sin of David. In 2 Samuel 12, after David had committed the great sin, the Lord sent the prophet to him to convince him of his sin. Notice how he added to his sin in verses 7–9:

> Thus saith the LORD God of Israel, I anointed thee king over Israel, and I delivered thee out of the hand of Saul; and I gave thee thy master's house, and thy master's wives into thy bosom, and gave thee the house of Israel and of Judah; and if that had been too little, I would moreover have given unto thee such and such things. Wherefore hast thou despised the commandment of the LORD?

Oh, it was this that struck the heart of David. "I have sinned," said David.

In Nehemiah 9:25–26, you have a remarkable Scripture for this idea of setting the mercy of God before you: "So they did eat, and were filled, and became fat, and delighted themselves in thy great goodness. Nevertheless they were disobedient, and rebelled against thee, and cast thy law behind their backs, and slew thy prophets." Here is how their sin was multiplied: they were filled with good things, yet they were nevertheless disobedient. Oh, might this Scripture not be applied to many of you? The Lord has filled your houses with an abundance of mercies; you cannot look into any of your families without seeing mercy. Yet despite all this, your heart is carnal. You swear, keep company with those who are immoral, profane the Sabbaths, and neglect the worship of God in your family. You have become an unclean wretch, disregarding all those mercies by which the Lord would woo you to obedience. That's the second thing that shows the necessity of learning to be full: without this lesson, we shall be guilty of sinning against much mercy. Likewise, the mercy of God will serve no other purpose than to add to our sin.

3. *If men do not learn how to be full, they will grow extremely wicked.* Though we already discussed how fullness fuels our lusts, I mention it briefly here to show how necessary it is that we learn how to be full in order to prevent us from becoming abominably wicked. Sin will become sinful beyond measure if we do not learn

how to be full. It is like a man with a weak body and poor health; if he has a full table and a strong appetite, he will become quite unhealthy if he does not learn how to control his diet. So it is with you; if your heart is weak (or worse), and you come to have a full condition, you are likely to become extremely spiritually unhealthy if do not know how to control yourself.

Therefore you find in Scripture that those who were in a full condition but lacked the grace to know how to be full are described as being the most wicked people in the world. Job 21:14 says, "Therefore they say unto God, Depart from us; for we desire not the knowledge of thy ways." And in Psalm 73 you may read at length of the prosperity of the wicked. And in Isaiah 2:7–8 we read, "Their land also is full of silver and gold, neither is there any end of their treasures; their land is also full of horses, neither is there any end of their chariots." Then notice verse 8: "Their land also is full of idols." These two things are linked together in this passage: prosperity and idolatry. Oh, and so it can be said of many families: "This family is full of all material goods, and yet it's also a family full of sin." Or, "Here's a man who is full of wealth, and yet he's a man who is just as full of sin as he is of wealth." If you do not learn how to abound, you will certainly abound in sin. Therefore, it is an absolutely necessary lesson for us to learn how to abound.

4. If you do not learn how to abound, your portion will be in this life. Unless the grace of God accompanies your abundance to teach you how to abound, you will be one of those whom God has said will have no other portion from Him in this world. If the Lord gives a man an estate and does not along with that give him some proportionate measure of grace to know how to use it and abound in it, God will say of him, "His portion shall be in this world." It's as if God says from heaven about this man, "Here's someone whose portion is in this world."

In Psalm 17:14, the psalmist speaks of men who have their portion in this world. Here is their consolation: "If you have a full estate, and if God gives you nothing else along with your full estate, it is likely to be all you get." You will ask, "Is this really such an important point?" Yes! For it would be ten thousand times better if you had never been born, even if you had a thousand times more in this world than you now have, if it proved to be your portion, your all. You are made for eternity, and those created things were not. Therefore, if your hope is in this world only, you are a wretched creature. Didn't Paul say that if our hope is only in this life, we are the most miserable of all men (1 Cor. 15:19)? I must say, if you have hope only in this life, you are the most miserable of all creatures, except for the devils themselves.

Oh, it is a dreadful thing for men or women to have their portion only in this world; yet this is exactly what they have, who have a great deal in this world but don't know how to use it for God. Consider this, you to whom God has given a greater portion than others. Do you think this way in the night: "Lord, Thou hast indeed made my condition more comfortable than others; I am fully supplied and have a steady means of income. But Lord, what if it turns out that my portion is only here?"

I remember it was said of Pope Gregory that he professed that there was no Scripture that struck his heart as much as this one: "But woe unto you that are rich! For ye have received your consolation" (Luke 6:24). He feared that his portion would be only here. The truth is that Scripture (along with the other in Psalm 17) should cut to the hearts of rich men and of those who have a full estate in this world. That is, it should go to their hearts unless their consciences tell them that, through the grace of God, they have learned in some measure how to use it as much for the glory of God as for their own comfort.

You consider it a bad thing for a man to have an estate and yet not know how to use it wisely for himself. Likewise, if a man who is born with a great inheritance turns out to be a fool, you know that he will squander his estate. Isn't it also a great evil for someone to possess a large estate and yet not know how to use it for God? Is it only an excellent thing to know how to use an estate and improve it for your own advantage, but not so excellent a thing to improve it for God? Oh, this is a miserable condition for any man to be in, to be full but not know how to be full. Such a man is likely to have his portion in this world.

5. If God has given you a measure of wealth and you do not know how to be full, then all that you have is cursed to you. There is a secret curse of God that goes along with this. For example, when a man gives something to someone out of anger or resentment, he might say, "Here, take it if you will; I hope you choke on it!" Men talk like this when they give things out of anger. But if you give something to your children out of love, you not only give it to them, but if there is any danger in it, you are careful to teach them to use it rightly. In the same way, when God gives things to His own people, He cares about them after He has given it. "I will give it to them," He says, "but I am concerned that this might turn out to their hurt."

But when God gives to a wicked man, He says, "Take them if you will." God never minds them any further; He never looks after them to see whether what they've received does them good or not. He never minds them but allows them to take such things and spoil themselves with them. He is not concerned. Wouldn't it be a sign of hatred toward a man if I handed a madman a sword? I could be guilty of murder. Yet it is as great an argument that God hates a man when He gives him an estate and yet does not give him a heart to use it properly. He puts, as it were, a sword into a madman's hand. But although I would not be just in doing so, yet God would be just, for He would do so as a punishment of sin.

And then it is put even more strongly in Psalm 69:22–23. In that passage you see how an abundance of outward comforts may be given as a curse to men; it is threatened as a punishment for their sin: "Let their table become a snare before them: and that which should have been for their welfare, let it become a trap." This is a terrifying text. It is a prophecy against those who gave Christ gall for His food and vinegar when He was upon the cross; it therefore becomes a curse against all those who cast insults at God's people in their affliction. Such men will add to the affliction of God's people when they are full and rich and prosperous in the world, so God pronounces this curse upon them: "Let their table become a snare before them: and that which should have been for their welfare, let it become a trap."

You have a table that is well furnished, but how do you know that it is nothing more than a snare for you, and a trap? We set traps to catch vermin. In the same way, God looks upon you as but vermin if you have a wicked heart and sets this to be a trap with which to catch you. Perhaps you do not see it. Well, then, pay attention to the words that follow: "Let their eyes be darkened, that they see not." This is a part of the curse. Few men see a curse upon their tables, but I tell you that this is part of God's curse upon them, that they should not see. Oh, what a great need there is, that we who have any fullness of God's gifts should learn how to be full; otherwise, that which should have been for our welfare turns into a curse for us. But a wicked man will be content as long as he may still enjoy what he has, even if it becomes a curse.

6. *If you have not learned to be full, this reveals the evil condition of your heart.* God may therefore justly, in His wrath, take away from you whatever you have because you do not know how to use it. It is like what any of you would do if you had a servant or anyone else in your house that had a knife in his hand. If you saw he was ready to do mischief with it, you would snatch it from him, saying, "No, if you do not know how to use it, you shall no longer have it." God is just to come upon you in His wrath and take away all your outward comforts, because you do not know how to use them. If you don't know how to make use of a child for God or an estate for God, He may therefore justly take them from you, since you don't know how to use them.

So God says in Psalm 78:25, "Man did eat angels' food: he sent them meat to the full." And in verse 29 He says, "So they did eat, and were well filled: for he gave them their own desire." But then verses 30–31 follow: "They were not estranged from their lust. But while the meat was yet in their mouths, the wrath of God came upon them." They ate to the fullest and had enough; but they were only greedily seeking to satisfy themselves. Therefore the wrath of God came upon them while the meat was still in their mouths. It provokes God's wrath upon men when they have fullness but have not learned how to be full.

And just as God may justly take it all away from them, He may also bring them into affliction. Oh, how sad it will be for them if they have not learned how to be full. Oh, then that will be something for their consciences to chew on, something that will terrify their souls. Afflictions will be dreadful to those who have had a full estate and have not learned to be full. Their conscience will upbraid them, saying, "Oh, you once had plenty; you once had comforts to the fullest. But how did you use them? What glory did God have by them? Did you not simply use them to fuel your lusts? Did you not make them serviceable to your own wickedness? And now it is righteous for God to take these things from you; these sorrows that are now upon you are but the beginning of sorrows." Oh, the conscience of a man who has been rich and afterward loses his estate! If he was not godly when he was rich, his conscience will tear him apart. Though now you enjoy your fullness, you may not expect to always enjoy it. What do you think will become of you when your fullness is taken away from you? Oh, then it will be terrible to you.

7. *If a man is in a full condition but does not learn how to be full, he will do a great deal of harm in the place where he lives, not only to himself but to others.* Oh, the evil he might do in a family, town, or country. One rich man may do

more mischief than a hundred other wicked men, if God does not cleanse his heart and sanctify his estate. God is not as concerned at the harm that vile drunkards can do, who go up and down from one bar to another; such men may destroy their own souls but do little harm to others. But oh, the hurt that comes from a man who has some means in the place where God has set him yet spends his nights in immorality and wantonness or condemns the ways of God and religion. Oh, the guiltiness that will come upon his spirit from such ways! Oh, how the gospel is hindered by such men, who have outward prosperous estates, yet despite that do not have hearts to make use of it. By contrast, as I will show shortly, it will be quite different with those who *have* learned how to be full. I mention this now to show the danger of a full condition so that if you are not someone who has learned how to be full, you may plead with God to teach you how to be full. Then, if He grants you a full condition, you will not contract the guilt of the sins of thousands of others upon you.

8. *If you are an unbeliever you cannot learn how to be full, and your full estate will endanger your salvation exceedingly.* Christ says, "It is easier for a camel to go through the eye of a needle, than for a rich man to enter into the kingdom of God" (Mark 10:25). Now Christ tells us what a rich man is: one who trusts in his riches (v. 24). The fullness of a man's condition endangers his salvation quite a bit if God does not teach him how to be full.

9. Not learning how to be full will make death more terrible for you. Oh, how terrible will death be to a man who has not learned to be full! Death comes, and it deprives him of everything. He must bid an everlasting farewell to his house and estate and to any land he may have gotten. Never has someone had such cheerful get-togethers as he used to have, but now those days are gone. They have come to an end, and he shall never have them anymore. Then death will trouble him, and his conscience will indeed terrify him. If he is in an afflicted condition, death will indeed terrify him, but when he sees that he must bid an everlasting farewell to all those things, then death will terrify him exceedingly. His conscience will tell him, "Now you are going to give an account before the great God for all those things that you enjoyed in this world." What a sad message this will be to some who are full. You think that because you have money to pay for what you eat and drink and enjoy, you will be called to no further account. Oh yes, you must be called to an account for all the things that you enjoy. Now if some men can scarcely count the mercies that they enjoy, then how will you who are full be able to give an account for them? I say all this to simply awaken the hearts of people who have the comforts of this world so that they may not simply be satisfied with what they enjoy, but will rather seek to learn to be full.

CHAPTER 5

The Excellency of Learning to Be Full

The excellency of learning to be full is very great. There are several ways in which this excellency can be seen.

1. It shows great nobility in the heart of a man. This nobility can be seen in two respects: first, because it demonstrates that this man is not just looking out for his own good. It's a sign of a disgraceful spirit when someone uses others to serve himself, but fails to care for others when he is able to do so. By contrast, it's a sign of a noble spirit when someone is careful to return proportionate respect to those who were helpful to him when he is able to do so. So it is with those who have learned to be full; they have noble spirits and are as careful to return proportionate respects to God as they are to receive any mercy from Him. Their nobility is further shown in this: they are thankful. A noble heart is a thankful heart that loves to acknowledge whenever it has received any mercy.

Second, it is a sign of a noble heart for one to be moved to duty by good and to be moved by mercy. It's a slavish spirit that is moved only by necessity and force and violence. It's nothing for a man to be forced to do a duty. By a whip, the lowest slave will be put to do that which is his duty, but for one to be wrought upon by love and goodness is a mark of true nobility. If the Lord has given you an estate, and you find that it draws your heart to God more and works upon your heart so that your affections are stirred by God's mercy, oh, this is a sign of a noble heart.

2. *Whatever grace such a man has is much more evident than other men's graces and is more beautiful.* A diamond set in a crown of gold sparkles more gloriously than when it is wrapped up in a dirty rag. So the graces of many who are poor and lowly in the world are obscured; they are (as it were) wrapped up in a dirty rag—just as sometimes they wrap up their dirty money. But as for a man who is eminent in the world—and godly too—his graces are like diamonds in a crown, as it were, that are so obvious before the world that the world takes notice of them and gives glory to God for them.

3. *It is an excellency because it is so rare.* It is a very rare thing for a man to be instructed in this lesson of being full. One of our early church fathers used to say that for a man not to become puffed up when he is put in a

high position is very unusual; the more unusual something is, the more glorious it is. It is a very rare blessing of God upon a man when that man learns how to be full. Where is the man who is able to withstand the temptations of prosperity? Such a man is hard to find. If adversity has slain her thousands, prosperity has slain her ten thousands. It is a rare virtue to have honor coupled with humility, and because it is so rare, that makes it all the more glorious.

I remember it was once said of a man who had been advanced to a position of great favor that his promotion did not succeed his former state, but rather was added to his former state. With most men, their promotion succeeds their former state—that is, the nobility of their character is left behind, along with their former position. But some men are not like that. Some are able to continue in the state they were in before—that is, their former humility, heavenly-mindedness, and holiness remain even after their promotion. Yes, this is an excellency indeed when a man's fullness is added to his former condition and does not succeed it; that is, he is the same man now that he was before. That's a rare blessing of God upon someone.

4. It is proof that someone is strong in grace when he is full and has learned how to be full—that is, how to be moderate in his prosperity. It is not only proof of grace in his life, but proof of the strength of his grace—just as a man who is able to tolerate much wine and yet refrains from getting drunk demonstrates proof of the strength of his body. Some think that they may take liberty to drink as much wine as they please, as long as they do not stagger in the streets. But you know that the prophet Isaiah says, "Woe unto them that are mighty to drink wine" (Isa. 5:22). It's a well-known saying that moderation is a sign of a strong heart. In the same way, moderation in the midst of prosperity is a sign of a strong heart.

It's a sign that God has given you strength of grace if your conscience can say to you, "Well, through God's mercy, though I have many weaknesses and often fail in what I do, yet I can say to the praise of God that my estate has not estranged my heart from God. Rather, my heart cleaves to God, and I have communion with God in the things that God sends me. And when God gives me profitable trips, I find my heart in the best temper, and I have sweeter communion with God than at other times." Can you say so? I appeal to your consciences now: Can you say, in the presence of God, "I never found my heart in a more heavenly spiritual temper than when I have found God blessing me in my labors, and I have enjoyed God in them." If you can say so, be of good comfort; you have learned a lesson that is worth a thousand times more than all your prosperity. This is your excellency: not that you have a fuller estate than others but that God has taught you such a lesson as this.

5. A person who has learned to be full is in a position to do a great deal of good. What an abundance of glory God may have from just one man in this way! By contrast, a man who is of a high state, and does not have grace along with it, is like an elder tree in the midst of a garden. Such a tree spoils the flowers and does much harm there. Yes, but someone who has an estate and is rich, and is also godly, stands as a prime flower in the garden and adds to its beauty. Commonly, you set a prime flower in the midst of a flower arrangement to be an ornament to all the rest. So also the Lord will have some to be rich, that they may be an ornament and a shelter to His servants.

Many, many hundreds of people will thank God for giving such men wealth, setting them in a position to provide for others. We say that the wealth of some men is well bestowed on them, for they do a lot of good with it. But when they go beyond this, when their hearts are set to use their estates for the furtherance of the gospel, for the beating down of sin, and for the support of religion, then all the people of God that live around them will praise God. Oh, for such a man! God has often in the past used such men, endowing them with large estates and stirring their hearts to provide for those who preached the gospel. If not for these men, what would have become of the gospel? Religion might have been trampled underfoot.

Won't this be a greater comfort in the day of Jesus Christ, to hear Christ acknowledge this and say, "I gave you an estate in the world, and I acknowledge that you made use of it for My glory and for religion. I made you an instrument to uphold these in the place where you were used." Oh, if Christ would say this, wouldn't it be worth a thousand times more to you than your estates?

6. *When it comes time for you to die, oh how sweetly you will die when you can say, "Oh, Lord, remember me for this good."* Nehemiah did this very thing at the end of his book. Look at the last words of Nehemiah. He was a man who was full of outward blessings, and he improved them for God's purposes. The very last thing he said was, "Remember me, O my God, for good" (Neh. 13:31). You likewise could say the same thing when it comes time for you to die if you use what you have for God's glory and for the furtherance of the gospel. Your conscience will not upbraid you as others' will. When they come to God for mercy, He will say, "What? Come to Me for mercy? I have bestowed you with much mercy already, and how did you abuse it? What expression can you use to cry out to Me for mercy when you have abused the mercy I've already given you?" Oh, but when your consciences can affirm to you that you have *not* abused God's mercy, but rather His mercy in outward things has drawn your hearts to Him and you have used them for His service, then you may, with joy and encouragement, say, "Remember me, O my God, for good."

7. If God should ever bring afflictions into your life, you would find sweetness and comfort in the fact that you have used your prosperity well. There will be no fear that adversity or afflictions will harm you if you have first learned how to use your prosperity. If you can deliver yourselves from the deceits of prosperity, it will not be very difficult to resist the temptations of adversity. Once a man has surrendered to God the comfort of his prosperity, God will take care to remove the gall and bitterness of his affliction. There is nothing more comfortable to a man in affliction than to consider that when he was prosperous he made use of it for the honor and glory of God. Such a man can say, "When I was in prosperity, God had honor; and now that I am in affliction, I can comfortably flee to God for peace and comfort to my soul."

8. This is the way that God attains His purpose and the purpose of His creatures. God achieves His purpose, the end goal of His works of creation and providence, in a special way from these men. The Lord has made this world and filled it with an abundance of excellent things. But how shall God attain His end—that is, to have glory from the excellent things that He has made in the world? Most men take them and abuse them to God's dishonor; if not for some men who had hearts to give God the glory from their estates, why, God would have no glory from all His works. All His works would be to no purpose, as it were. But now it seems that God has called you out, to give Him the glory for His works.

You who are great landlords complain during a bad economy that you cannot receive your rents because your renters were never paid so little as they are now. But now ask this of yourselves: How well do you pay your rent to the Lord, from whom you have received all that you have? You highly esteem those renters who are reliable and punctual in paying their rent. Likewise, God highly esteems those who constantly render to Him the rent of praise and honor for the many enjoyments they have in this world. This cannot help but bring you a great deal of comfort and shows the excellency of learning how to be full.

Exhortation

I have just a few more points to open up regarding this lesson before we come to the application, although we have endeavored to apply it all along the way. Before doing that, though, let me close this chapter by exhorting you to let these things sink into your hearts. I'll give you one Scripture so that you may go out and seek God, asking Him to teach you how to be full and how to learn this lesson. Jude 12 says, "These are spots in your feasts of charity, when they feast with you, feeding themselves without fear." There is the description of wicked and ungodly men: they feast themselves without fear so that they may be fed to the full; they care about nothing else. Oh, this is a sign of a wretched, wicked man, to feast himself without fear. God has given you fullness of wealth, and for what? Do you consume it without fear?

If God has given you an estate, along with all the outward comforts in this world according to your heart's desire, you ought to be compelled to fear—fear that you might not improve it for God. Oh, that God would send you away from His presence with trembling hearts as you consider what you have heard. Let the husband repeat this to his wife, and the wife to her husband, when they see that God is supplying them with abundance: "The Lord has given us these outward comforts. He has given us more outward mercies than most other people. Oh, but if we do not improve them for God, if we abuse them, if we do not have proportionate grace to make use of them, what will become of us?" Now, having your hearts possessed with the fear of this, you will even more likely be driven to God in prayer, to seek for Him to instruct you in this lesson, to teach you how to be full.

CHAPTER 6

The Mystery of Learning to Be Full

There is a great mystery in learning how to be full. Just as there is a mystery of godliness in contentment, so there is a mystery in this. Although there are indeed some natural rules we may give to men to teach them how to make use of their prosperity, I want to go beyond that to show you that it is done in a mysterious way. We would all do very well if we were moved to learn this lesson by natural principles. But I will endeavor to go further than that with you; I want to show you how to learn to be full in a spiritual way, according to the rules of the gospel. I will show you how to manifest the mystery of godliness in giving God the glory of your estates and all your worldly comforts.

In *The Rare Jewel of Christian Contentment*, we considered this method in learning contentment in times of want: the mystery of godliness. I told you then that the word in Philippians 4:12, "I am instructed" (as it reads in your Bibles), in the original reads, "I am taught as in a mystery." Therefore, Paul is saying that there is a mystery in both of these lessons, in learning how to abound and how to suffer need. I have already detailed for you the many ways in which the mystery of godliness is key in learning how to be content. Likewise, a godly man knows how to abound in a different manner from any other man.

Perhaps a man by some strength of natural prudence and wisdom might learn how to order his estate so as not to be very inordinate and wicked in how he manages it. A man who has civility and natural wisdom may make some good use of the blessings God has given him, but a godly man is different. A godly man's heart goes further than natural wisdom is able to teach. He learns to sanctify the name of God in the estate and outward blessings he has received from God.

Grace will raise such a man's spirit higher than that of the natural man; it will do so in these ways.

1. *A godly man learns to abound by being faithful.* "A faithful man shall abound with blessings" (Prov. 28:20). Many think that the only way to gain an abundance is by being deceitful, by being shifty; they do not dare entrust themselves to the ways of faithfulness. They see a mighty current of opposition against them. By contrast, the godly man desires neither to gain more nor to enjoy more in this world than he may acquire by being faithful.

2. *A godly man learns how to be full by regularly surrendering up his estate, his comforts, and his possessions*

to God. He learns how to enjoy these things by surrendering them to God. This is a way that a natural man understands little of—to know how to enjoy his comforts by surrendering them up—yet that is the way of a gracious heart. Very frequently, when he gets alone in his closet, he surrenders up his belongings, saying, "Lord, Thou hast blessed me with many outward comforts—more than Thou hast done for others among my brothers. Lord, I now profess that all of this is Thine; I give it all up to Thee. It all belongs to Thee, and I desire to enjoy it no further than is needed for me to be useful to Thee in the place where Thou hast set me. Lord, I surrender myself and all my fullness to Thee. Take it all; it is at Thy disposal. Use it for Thine own praise and glory." Once he has done this, he actually enjoys more sweetness than he would in any other way. It is not by greedy use that he learns to enjoy his fullness, but by surrendering up what he has to God. By doing so, he comes to enjoy his fullness in a better manner and more comfortably than he ever did before.

A godly heart finds this out by experience. A godly heart discovers that the more often anything comes from God's hand, the better and sweeter it is. Therefore, he is willing to regularly give up what he has into God's hand. A man who can just as easily resign everything up to God as he can receive anything from God and does so freely and cheerfully is the only man who is blessed in what he enjoys in this world.

3. A godly man learns how to be full in this mysterious way: he seeks to preserve his comforts and enrich himself by sharing what he has. That is, he seeks to preserve his comforts, not only by surrendering them to God but also by sharing them. He seeks to enrich himself by sharing his riches. Although this is mysterious, the Scriptures clearly show that this is the way of a gracious heart. A person with a carnal heart enjoys his fullness, but how does he do it? He does it by keeping it to himself. Yes, but one with a godly heart, one that learns by way of mystery how to be full, sees that the only way to preserve his estate is by sharing it with others, by doing many good works, and by making good use of his estate. He sees that he must use his possessions for the public good, for the glory of God, and for the good of his brothers. This is a mystery to the world.

There is a noteworthy Scripture in Isaiah 32 that shows this to be the way a godly man preserves his estate. Verse 8 says, "But the liberal deviseth liberal things." Notice that he does not give liberally only when he is presented with the opportunity to do so; rather, he studies within his own heart to devise and plan ways to share his wealth for the good of others. "Yes," you will say, "but he may quickly give it all away and grow to be a beggar himself." No, observe what the text says: "And by liberal things shall he stand." That is how he preserves what he has: he entrusts it with God. Indeed, he will be able to enjoy the comforts of his life by sharing them with others. In that way, he seeks to get riches by the sharing of his riches.

The Scripture that you have for this is 1 Timothy 6:17–18: "Charge them that are rich in this world, that they be not high-minded, nor trust in uncertain riches, but in the living God, who giveth us richly all things to enjoy; that they do good, that they be rich in good works, ready to distribute." The more good works he does, the richer he accounts himself to be. He considers it to be greater gain to part with anything in order to do good with it than to keep it for himself.

Now ordinarily a man with a carnal heart, when he is called to do good works, cannot help but do something out of shame. Yes, but he thinks he is the poorer for it. "What? Will you take away all my estate and make me a beggar? These frequent contributions draw away from my estate!" They think that so much giving draws their heart-blood away, so they grow poorer and poorer. But a godly man sees it this way: the more good works he does, the richer he becomes. This is a way to become truly rich, a way with which the world is unacquainted: be rich in good works. The more one engages in good works, the richer he is.

Even God Himself accounts His riches to be in the works of mercy. In Ephesians 2:7 you will find that the riches of God are in His works of mercy, "that in the ages to come he might shew the exceeding riches of his grace in his kindness toward us through Christ Jesus." God is not said to be rich in power so much as He is said to be rich in grace, in the works of mercy, and in the works of kindness. Therefore a godly man, who has learned by the grace of God how to be full, accounts himself to be made rich by sharing whatever fullness God has given him, for the glory of His name and for the good of others. The apostle Paul uses this argument to motivate men to give their possessions for the good of others: "God is able to make all grace abound toward you; that ye, always having all sufficiency in all things, may abound to every good work" (2 Cor. 9:8). This is the third mysterious way of a godly man's learning how to be full.

4. *A godly man learns how to be full in this mysterious way: he learns how to have comfort in his riches by putting his affections for those riches to death.* A godly man moderates his spirit in the joy he receives from what God has given him; in that way he receives greater joy from them. This, you will say, is a riddle: How can a man have greater joy in outward things by moderating his joy and have a greater fullness in his abundance by keeping himself within bounds? Yet this is the way of a godly man: the more he keeps himself within bounds, the more comfort he has in his abundance. And the more he can put his affections for worldly comforts to death, the more comfort he actually receives from these comforts.

Now, because this may seem to be a great riddle and mystery (for so it is), I will give you one Scripture that will spell it out fully. It is in Philippians 4:4: "Rejoice in the Lord always: and again I say, Rejoice." Here the apostle calls people to rejoice, and rejoice in the Lord—that is, to rejoice not only in spiritual things but also in all of God's blessings in a spiritual way. Now the men of the world, when they are called to rejoice, and again to rejoice, think they know how to rejoice only if they let their hearts out fully to something without any restrictions; they do not know how to keep within any boundaries.

But mark the words that follow: "Let your moderation be known unto all men" (v. 5). It is as if the apostle said, "If you would indeed truly rejoice, graciously and fully, I exhort you to rejoice, and again to rejoice." Such words are pleasing to the heart of a man. "We will give ourselves liberty to rejoice, and we will enlarge ourselves in our joy." "Yes," says the apostle, "but let your moderation be known to all men."

By adding this exhortation, "let your moderation be known to all men," it is apparent that he is referring to the joy we take in outward things as well as spiritual things. In saying "let your moderation be known to all," he does not forbid you to rejoice in your belongings. You may rejoice in the comforts of this world that God has given you. But if you would have true joy, the kind that would truly gladden your hearts, let your moderation be known to all men. Control yourselves in your joy, and let your hearts be deadened to the world so that you may rejoice in God, even while you rejoice in the outward blessings that He has given you.

Although many men may think this is a mystery, and hardly believable, yet those who are truly godly find this to be true by experience. I appeal to you: When have you had the greatest comfort and joy in your estate and income, except for those times when your hearts have been mortified to the world and when you were able to keep yourselves within limits? If a man goes abroad and among company and can keep his appetite in bounds and eat moderately, he has more comfort in his food and drink than another man does who eats excessively. A man who eats and drinks moderately preserves his health, and by preserving his health he enjoys more sweetness in his food and drink than those who eat and drink immoderately.

When a man has been abroad among company and lets out his heart profusely to laughter and merriment, he pins all his joy upon his merriment. But even in the midst of his laughter his heart is sad, and when he comes home, he comes home with a dead spirit. He is like Nabal. You know that while he was feasting his heart was merry, but as soon as his drunkenness was gone from him, his heart died like a stone (1 Sam. 25:37). Many spend their time keeping company with those who are immoral, giving themselves liberty in jolliness and mirth, yet the next day they find that their hearts are as dead as stone. Further, their spirits come under a great deal of guilt, and their consciences fly in their faces so that they do not have as much joy in their spirits as those who can keep themselves within bounds.

However, those who can go in a sober way and meet with their neighbors and rejoice with one another can bless God when they come home for this refreshing time they have had. And the next morning, their hearts are in a sweet and joyful frame. The more we keep ourselves in bounds in the use of created things, the more comfort we have in using them. That's the fourth mysterious way a godly man's heart learns how to abound: he learns how to enjoy the world by deadening his affections to it and by keeping himself within bounds in the use of created things.

5. *Another mysterious way a godly person learns how to abound is this: by sanctifying all that he has by the Word and prayer.* Remember, one of the ways of knowing how to be in want is by having our afflictions sanctified to us. It is also the way to learn how to abound. People with carnal hearts have little skill in this. They think they know how to abound by their natural wisdom. Yes, but the way a godly heart uses for abounding is this: "God has prospered me in my life in many different ways; now let me go to God and exercise faith in His Word and seek Him in prayer, that I may have a sanctified use of all these things God has granted me."

First Timothy 4:4–5 says that everything created by God is good, and nothing is to be refused if it is received with thanksgiving, "for it is sanctified by the word of God and prayer." Allow me to open up this Scripture a little: How is it sanctified by the Word? When the apostle speaks of sanctifying by the Word, his intent is this: a godly man has another kind of interest in created things than other men have. He is saying, "All things are good, but how shall they be good to me? How will I know they are good to me? It must be by the Word. I cannot know that they are good to me, in order for me to have a sanctified use of them, unless I enjoy them as useful for God and to further eternal good." For that is how we know that something has been sanctified, when it has been consecrated, as it were, and made holy: when it is made useful to the highest and ultimate purpose.

A place is said to be sanctified when it is separated from other things for God; so also the blessing of God is upon all my possessions, upon all that I own, when it all works for God's glory and my ultimate good. That is when it becomes truly sanctified to me.

Now, how does this come about? It is by the Word of God. There are two portions of the Word through which this takes place.

First, through the Word of the gospel, which reveals the restoration of my right to an even higher title than I ever had in Adam, though this right had previously been forfeited due to my sin. Because of our fall into sin, we have lost all our rights to enjoy created things for our outward comfort. Now God indeed does, out of His bounty, give to some men abundance here in this world. He gives them those things that are in themselves good. Yes, but how will these things become good to him? It must be by the Word, God says. God uses the Word of His gospel, the covenant He has made with His poor servants in Christ as revealed in His Word, to give the godly man a sanctified use of what He has.

The second portion of the Word by which our possessions become sanctified is by the promises in the Word. The promises in Scripture give nothing to us without first attaching a blessing to it. If indeed I had whatever I enjoy in a merely natural way, by way of general providence, I could not expect any such blessing. If I enjoy it in a merely natural way, it may actually prove to be a curse to me. If I enjoy it merely by God's general providence, it is not a sanctified use. But now that I enjoy all that I have through my understanding of the Word, I enjoy it in a spiritual way; everything becomes sanctified to me.

If a man appreciates what he has through the lens of the Word of the promise or by the Word of the gospel, where Jesus Christ is revealed to us, his ability to profit from the things he enjoys becomes transformed by Jesus Christ, the Word who sanctifies everything to us.

Of all men, those who are well off and have important titles have the most reason to be familiar with the Scriptures. It would be a sad accusation upon any of you who have so much in this world that you have no Bibles on your bookshelves or that you seldom open them up.

Most men regard the things they enjoy only by way of God's general providence; one with a godly heart, however, views these things through the Word of God. That is what gives him a sanctified use of such things. Through the power of the Word he learns how to be full and to use all his abundance in a right way. The way he chooses to use his fullness when God blesses him is to increase his faith in the Word of the gospel, that is, in the promise of eternal life. He uses his fullness to better appreciate God's covenant with man through Jesus Christ. Godliness has the promise of the things of this life and of that which is to come (1 Tim. 4:8). If God is able to provide such things here and now, He is certainly able to provide for our eternal happiness. So a godly man trusts in God's promise, and he uses what he has already received to strengthen his faith in what is to come. In this way, he develops a sanctified use and improvement of all the good things that he enjoys in this world.

How are the things God has created sanctified by prayer? This is, I suppose, easier for you to understand. That is, when I receive any good from any created thing, then I am to seek God in prayer, that I may have a sanctified use of it. A godly man never prays more than when God prospers him in this world. Carnal men will pray much in times of affliction, but to be motivated to pray by prosperity is rare. The more any man has, the more need he has to pray; therefore, rich men need to pray more than poor men. Few of you think so, and even fewer do so. True, the Scripture does say, "In their affliction they will seek me early" (Hos. 5:15). Yes, but that might be a sign of a merely carnal heart. By contrast, a godly man, when God prospers him, sees cause to pray the most then.

If this is true, it is certainly a mystery. Isn't it a mystery to most rich men? Do their riches compel them to pray more than before and to exercise faith in the Word more than before? They instead reason with themselves, saying that it is for poor people, who have nothing in the world, to live by faith. They think that it is fitting for them to believe and trust in God. But a godly man will exercise more faith when he has the most in the world. That is a good way to consider this mystery of knowing how to be full.

6. *A further way in the mystery of knowing how to be full is this: a person with a godly heart, because of his fullness, increases in humility.* He grows sensible of his unworthiness by his fullness. Now this is a way of mystery too. It is a good thing for a man to have humility together *with* his fullness, but to have humility *because of* his fullness is a very great mystery. It is a rare thing to see humble prosperity, but to see a man humbled *by* his prosperity is rare indeed. Affliction will humble men; that is true, and everyone can understand that. But how prosperity can humble men is very hard to understand.

I'll give you a scriptural example from 2 Samuel 7:18 of how prosperity will humble a gracious heart.

There, the Lord told David of great things He would do for him and spoke to him of the honor that He had put upon him. He further told David how He would continue his line as a great line and as an honorable lineage, like the great men of the earth. Notice this: one would have thought the heart of David would have become puffed up with pride when God told him not only of the great things He had done, but also the great things He would do. That would have puffed up a carnal heart. But read verses 18–22:

> Then went king David in, and sat before the Lord, and he said, Who am I, O Lord God, and what is my house, that thou hast brought me hitherto? And this was yet a small thing in thy sight, O Lord God; but thou hast spoken also of thy servant's house for a great while to come. And is this the manner of man, O Lord God? And what can David say more unto Thee? For thou, Lord God, knowest thy servant. For thy word's sake, and according to thine own heart, hast thou done all these great things, to make thy servant know them. Wherefore thou art great, O Lord God.

David does not bless himself, saying, "Oh, God has made me great." Rather, he says, "Wherefore thou art great," "Who am I?" and "What is my house?" He says that it is "according to thine own heart," implying that it is not according to anything in him. The more God told him about the great things he had and would have, the more humble David's heart was.

Oh, this is a sign of true humility, when you find your income to be more than it had been previously (such as when you have a successful trip and gain a great amount of income) and then to get alone, as it is said that David did, and sit down before the Lord. Go and set yourself before the Lord and fall down; humble your soul, saying, "Oh, Lord, who am I, that Thou shouldest deal so graciously with me and that Thou shouldest make such a difference between me and others?"

Landlords, when you receive your rents each quarter, you may be getting more than others receive. When this happens, think to yourself, "Lord, what is it that has made the difference between me and others? Others have a meager daily income with which to provide for their families, and Thou hast given me a hundred times more. Oh, Lord, what am I, that it should be like this with me more than with others?" Oh, if you responded this way, it would be right indeed, for this is the way a godly man learns how to be full. His fullness teaches him humility. By learning humility from his fullness, he comes to know how to be full for the glory of God and the good of His church.

7. *Another mystery in a godly man's learning how to be full is this: he accounts it to be better to lose for God, and return to God, than to gain for himself, and keep to himself.* When a godly man comes to have a full condition, he rejoices in his outward blessings according to how

God would have him do so. Yes, but he rejoices more in the fact that he has something to venture and to lose for God than the fact that he has gain for himself. While one man rejoices that he has an estate by which he may live happily and without worries in the world, the other man rejoices that he has an estate that he may venture for God. He accounts it a greater privilege to return anything to God than to receive from God. This is a mystery too.

8. *Though a godly man sees himself as being unworthy of the smallest part of anything good he has, his heart is nevertheless raised, in a holy way, above all his abundance.* He judges himself to be unworthy of the smallest crumb, yet he views all the created things in heaven and earth as being too low to satisfy him, to be his portion. This is a mystery. The only man who knows how to abound in a spiritual way is the one who is able to rise above all his abundance. A heart full of grace lies low under God and Christ; the lower he lies, the more he has. He places all the pomp and glory of the world under his feet. How great is this mystery of godliness!

9. *This mystery of abounding is further seen in this: a godly man learns how to abound by abounding in holiness.* The more he abounds in worldly riches, the more he seeks to abound in holiness and in the duties of God's worship. This is indeed a mystery to the men of the world.

They think that poor men, who do not have so much to do in the world, may regularly attend the worship of God and hear sermons and meditate and so forth. However, they think that it cannot be expected from them because they have so much that takes them away from such things. By contrast, godliness will teach men to abound in their many businesses, in their outward prosperity, and in the great things of the world by adding a proportionate abundance in both the performance of the worship of God and in holiness.

Some think that because they have so many things to draw their attention away, they cannot be as holy as others. But godliness will teach them to be more holy, according to the proportion of their estate. As those who are eminent above others, so they will labor that their holiness shall be eminent above others. Oh, this would be an excellent thing indeed, if all rich men would never satisfy themselves only with having more than others have but would consider the degree to which God has placed their status higher above others and endeavor to be above others in holiness to the same degree. Imagine if all rich men were never satisfied until they attained such eminence in holiness. For men to do this is a mysterious thing. Wherever this can be found, you will certainly find those who have been well instructed in the mystery of godliness.

10. A final way is this: a man who has learned to abound is as aware and sensible of his dependence on God in the

height of his prosperity as he is in the depth of his adversity. Therefore even noblemen and princes, if Christ has taught them this lesson, will come daily to God's gate in prayer to beg for their daily bread.

Therefore you see that a godly heart learns how to abound, not in a merely natural way (that is, by natural wisdom), but in a way of mystery and godliness.

CHAPTER 7

Lessons for Learning to Be Full

There are several specific lessons for a godly man if he is to learn how to abound. Just as I told you in knowing how to be content one needs to learn a great many lessons before he gets to be instructed in the art of contentment in affliction, so it is true with the art of abounding. Let me just mention several of these things.

1. He must learn the lesson of this principle: knowing the Source from where all his good comes; knowing the Fountain from where all his good springs. Be thoroughly instructed in that. I enjoy this and that outward comfort, but from where have I gotten them? You may say, "God has blessed my endeavors and skills in that He has given me more than others. Yes, but it is the blessing of God in all this that goes beyond my skill. Perhaps you have had friends or family that have died and left certain things to you, such as property or money. It is true that they left you those things, but the Fountain is on high, from where all the outward good that I have comes.

Most people generally acknowledge this, but the learning of it in a truly godly manner will work mightily upon the heart—that is, the understanding that God is the fountain of all my outward, as well as my spiritual, good.

2. *He must learn the lesson of the fear of God.* In Deuteronomy 6:11–12, God issues a warning to His people. He tells them that, in the midst of their enjoyment of all the many good things they were to receive, they must not forget Him. Then, in verse 13, He adds the way they could accomplish this: "Thou shalt fear the LORD thy God, and serve him." You should not be so presumptuous as to do whatever you wish; let the fear of God be upon you to keep you from pride, immorality, and licentiousness.

In Nehemiah 5, we read that Nehemiah had been raised to a position of honor. As such, he had as much power in his hands to impose his will on men as others in his position did; such men even made their servants lord their power over the people. "But so did not I," he said, "because of the fear of God" (v. 15). So those of you in positions of power ought to say, "Even if others abuse the power with which God has entrusted them, as for me, I will not do so; the fear of God is upon me. Regardless of what others in my position do, or have done, in abusing their power, God forbid that I should do so because I fear God."

3. We must understand that the very preservation of the world is through the mediation of Jesus Christ. The source of all our abundance is not only God, the First Being, the Creator of all in His providence; it is God in Christ. Without such a Redeemer, the world would fall apart all around us. All the good things in creation are preserved by the power of Christ now (Col. 1:17). So a person with a godly heart understands that as the Fountain of all, He is not only God the Creator of all, but God through Christ the Mediator, who preserves the world. The world would otherwise fall into confusion. Therefore, all the good that I have comes from God's wisdom and goodness, which has ordained that I have these things through Christ the Mediator.

4. We need to thoroughly learn the lesson of our unworthiness. You must learn that you are unworthy to receive the smallest crumb of bread or the least drop of water to cool you. We have spoken of this before in relation to contentment in times of want; however, understanding your own baseness and vileness before the Lord will also teach you how to abound.

I am not now telling you necessarily to learn your unworthiness *by* your prosperity; that was spoken of before, as being learned by way of mystery. Rather, I am now telling you this: learn it any way you can. Learn it by considering your own sinfulness, your inability to use those things you do have, and by considering how little service you have done for God. Learn to know yourselves. That was the lesson in learning how to be in want—to know yourselves. But rich men especially, above all other men, need to learn how to know themselves.

5. *Learn the vanity of created things, as well as the uncertainty of them.* Just as this will help you to learn how to be content in times of want, it will likewise help you to know how to abound. It's true, I have these things, but what are these things compared to an immortal soul? Isn't there a vanity in all these things in the world? They don't make me that different from others who don't have such things. In fact, they are the very same things someone who hates God may have. These very things are what a reprobate might have for his portion. That meditation will make men willing to be content, not only when they lack such things but also when they possess them in abundance.

Suppose I currently possess an abundance of these things. What great reason is there that my heart should be lifted up by that? Though there are many now in the world that may be lower than I am, there is also an abundance of souls in hell that had more than I have.

Oh, this will be a means to moderate your heart and help you know how to abound when you consider the vanity of the things of the world and the uncertainty of them. I have them now, but how quickly they may be gone! My house is magnificently furnished, but how quickly God may send a fire! Oh, consider the uncertainty of all that you have, and this will teach you how to make use of the things you have by holding them loosely. "Charge them that are rich in this world, that they be not highminded, nor trust in uncertain riches" (1 Tim. 6:17).

Even if God does not take away your riches, just let Him alter your health and bring some pain or disease. What good will all your riches do you then? Let God but touch me in my brain, and I will not know how to make use of my estate. Or, let Him but touch me in the body—a little in the kidneys or pain in the bowels— what is the world to me then? Oh, consider the vanity and the uncertainty of all things; learning this lesson is a great help in knowing how to abound.

6. *Another lesson that will teach men how to abound is to learn that all these things are only talents.* God gives them to me to trade them. I am only God's steward, and God charges me to trade for Him in all I do. This will teach men how to abound. When you hire someone to transact business on your behalf, he will—if he is faithful— consider this: "These are my master's goods, and I am but a steward; I am required to give an account, and therefore I must keep my books even." The consideration of this will take his thoughts off other things and make him consider his books, to keep them even.

Oh, if you would just learn this lesson, that all outward comforts are talents that are given to you to manage for God and that you are His stewards, it would make you keep the books even. Every day you would be checking the books, saying, "Are things even between God and me? What does God aim at? Why should I have a prosperous estate and not others?" By searching to learn God's purpose in doing so, a man's conscience will now tell him, "Surely God did not aim at this, that I should have more satisfaction for my flesh. There is something else that God was aiming at; let me learn to know God's end."

7. Learn that man is born to hard work, and even the greatest on the earth are not exempted. None of you are to live lazily, like the leviathan in the sea in Psalm 104:26; the psalmist says, "There is that leviathan, whom thou hast made to play therein." This is not the purpose for which you were made; neither is it the purpose for which your life continues. Not all hard work is servile, and though God may have fitted your noble spirit for other types of labor, He still created you for hard work.

8. A further lesson that would be a great help to you in learning how to abound is this: God very seldom entrusts His own people with these outward comforts. We spoke of this when we began, but now I bring it in as a lesson to be learned and to show you how that will help you to know how to abound. I spoke of it as evidence to show that it is a difficult thing for us to learn how to abound.

This lesson will compel us to learn to be much more watchful over ourselves.

9. *Learn the excellence of true riches, namely, spiritual riches.* Luther used to say that the smallest degree of grace, and every gracious work, is worth more than heaven and earth. He professed that he would rather understand one psalm than to have all the riches of the world. If we were taken up into heaven, the earth would seem very small to us, just like the stars seem small to us now. Those things that appear insignificant to us now have great significance from heaven's viewpoint.

10. *Learn that the least sin is a greater evil than all earthly prosperity can be good.* To commit any single sin brings upon you more misery than your honor and wealth can bring you happiness. If you were thoroughly instructed in this, then this would be your response:

+ You would take heed against obtaining or bestowing any riches or honors through any sinful means. Abraham would not let it be said of him that the king of Sodom made him rich (Gen. 14:21–23). So let it never be said of you that sin has made you rich or has preserved your wealthy condition.

+ If you have learned this lesson, then you will certainly restore to the utmost of your ability anything you have or shall get through any sinful means.

+ This would make you take heed of abusing your possessions as a means to sin. This lesson teaches you that you will do yourselves more hurt by one sin than all that you own in this world can do you any good.

There are a few concluding lessons that we need to learn if we are to be instructed in the art of abounding.

11. We are not to praise ourselves for our abundance.

12. We should desire a measure of grace proportionate to whatever we possess, so that whatever we have will not harm us rather than turning out for our good.

13. The final lesson to be learned is this: God has set this time of your life as the time to provide for eternity. This would make you see the need to be serious-minded. Instead of thinking that every serious thought is simply melancholy, this lesson will remove much of the vanity and frivolity from your spirits.

This would make you cautious of spending so much time in the use and enjoyment of the things of this world if they hinder you in the least in fulfilling the great work for which you live: the advancement of the gospel and your own spiritual good. Learning this lesson would move you to use all that you own, to the utmost of your ability, for these great purposes. In doing this, you will learn how to truly abound.

There are many other lessons that I could present to help us know how to abound. However, the truth is that almost everything that helps us know how to be in want will likewise help us know how to abound. Therefore I name only these things.

CHAPTER 8

Increasing the Guilt of Sins of Abundance

There have been times when God's sore displeasure has been shown against those who demonstrate extreme, unrestrained excess in the midst of their abundance. Such men run the good blessings of God into the dirt, using them only to satisfy their basest lusts. Let those of you who abound, therefore, take heed of this. This sin is in itself very great, but the contemptibility of this sin is increased greatly when the following conditions take place.

1. The first condition is when you abuse your wealth in light of the suffering of others. If you abuse your abundance while others suffer need—when thousands are ready to perish due to a lack of necessities—how great has your sin against God then become! It now becomes a loud cry in God's ears against you.

2. A second condition is when you abuse your wealth after God has raised you up from a poorer condition. When

God has raised you up from meager beginnings, His hand becomes even more remarkable when it emerges to give you abundance. How great, therefore, is your sin when you abuse this abundance!

3. *A third condition is when you abuse your wealth after God has preserved your riches through difficult times.* If your riches have passed through many difficulties and yet been preserved, so that even at times when you had given up hope and presumed that all was lost, God came in and caused your very full estate to continue, then consider this: What do you think was God's purpose in allowing it to continue? Was it so that you could have further opportunity to satisfy your lusts, to be hinderers of good, and to be promoters of evil in the places where you live? God forbid.

4. *A fourth condition is when you abuse your wealth while ignoring the prodding of your conscience.* If you still enjoy your worldly goods, despite the fact that your consciences accuse you of being guilty of greatly abusing them, it is a wonder that God has not violently torn it all away from you—or torn you away from it. Will you now continue to provoke God against you? Is your former abuse of such mercies not enough (or, rather, too much), that you will abuse them even further? May the Lord strike your hearts in this matter.

5. *A fifth condition is if you are abusing mercies that were previously taken away, but have now been restored to you.* If the mercies that you now have are renewed mercies— that is, mercies received after God has brought you low through terrible afflictions and then restored a great deal of it back to you again (or all of it, or even more than you had before)—will you now abuse His mercies again? What will be the expression on your face when you look upon God, when He calls you to account for this?

6. *A sixth condition is if you are using your wealth for selfishness rather than service.* If God gives you abundance while there are opportunities for great service, and rather than seizing that opportunity you care about nothing but satisfying your own lusts, living uselessly with all that abundance that God has given you, this is vile in God's eyes. If someone else had half the estate and means of doing good that you have, how useful would he be! God would have much service from him, and he would bless God for those opportunities that you don't even consider. Oh, that this might cause some misgiving thoughts to arise in you; if there is any light of conscience in you, may it wound your heart this day for this great sin of yours.

7. *A seventh condition is if you forget previous promises you made to God when your wealth was threatened.* Many of you have at one time or another solemnly promised

this to God: that if He would preserve your wealth or perhaps restore you to the enjoyment of it, you would render it back up to Him to honor Him with it. Many have done so, earnestly seeking God for their preservation and deliverance. However, if God does restore you again and you forget Him, know that you not only sin in doing this but also that this highly increases the degree of your guilt.

8. *A final condition is when you ignore the means of grace to help you honor God with your wealth.* If God not only gives you abundance but also gives you an abundance of the means of grace to help you learn how to abound, and yet despite this you still do not do so nor does it even enter your mind to do so, this also increases the guilt of your sin. If you lived in the former dark times, in times when the popes hid much of the light of the Word from the church, your guilt would not be so great, but since you live in such a time as now, when the means of grace abound, the guilt of your sin is raised very high.

CHAPTER 9

Applications for Improving Prosperous Conditions

We come now as briefly as we can to wind up this whole lesson with a word of application.

1. All that has been said up this point serves to rebuke those who are concerned only with learning how to gain abundance in the world but are not concerned with learning how to abound. Such people are never satisfied that they have enough, but learning how to use what they have for God and how to manage their fullness is scarcely in their thoughts. Remember Jude 12; among the several characteristics of a wicked man he gives, he adds that "they feast with you, feeding themselves without fear." In other words, a wicked man freely takes in the delights given by the Creator, but there is no fear that God will fail to receive the glory He deserves from it. This never even enters his mind at all.

I appeal to you in the name of God: Have these things that have been spoken to you been in your thoughts? I dare not overwhelm you by saying that every single particular point should be in your thoughts. But in general, has knowing how to honor God with your wealth been in your thoughts and concerns as much as knowing how to increase your wealth? God knows, as might your consciences, whether you have been more concerned with learning how to gain abundance than on learning how to abound. From what has been said out of the Scripture, has the Lord rebuked you for being one who has a carnal heart, a sensual and earthly heart, and who is little acquainted with the ways of God and with spiritual things? Oh, that you would examine your own soul in your quiet thoughts and meditations and that God would grip your hearts with what has been said regarding all this!

2. *We are taught what an excellent thing religion is; it helps us in every condition.* Religion helps us to know how to be in want; it also helps us to know how to abound. If we are in a lowly state, it provides the means to help us; if we are in a higher state, it provides another means to help us. Oh, religion is of admirable usefulness. Grace and godliness are useful, but in a different way than the world thinks they are. And though religion is useful to all men, it is above all greatly useful to rich men.

Oh, that rich men would believe that they have the greatest need of grace! Of all men, rich men ought to learn by this lesson to be in love with godliness and with the methods for receiving grace; there is nothing that can do them as much good as religion. If they had a measure of grace proportionate to their riches, then they would be happy men indeed! If the Lord would be pleased to add His upper springs of grace to His lower springs of blessing, then they would be happy creatures. God has given you an abundance of the lower springs, but has He given you the upper springs too? Oh, think this to yourselves: "The Lord has given me plenty for this world, to carry me through this pilgrimage of mine, but if I were to have grace added to all that I have, then I would be a happy man indeed!" Oh, learn to know how excellent grace is, and learn how greatly you, above all other men, have need for it.

Those of you in high positions or with honorable titles who have great estates to leave to your children: Do you desire that they have an upbringing suitable to the estates you intend to leave to them? How repulsive it is in the eyes of all men when someone has a great estate but a pitiful upbringing! He is a fool; he doesn't know how to manage his estate once he has it, and he quickly embezzles it all away. He becomes completely undone. Why should you, then, not consider it a great evil for you or your children to have estates and honors but then to have no skill in knowing how to use them for God and for the furtherance of your and their eternal good?

Only godliness, learned in Christ's school, teaches this. This is the most necessary upbringing one can have, and the most honorable. With as much as lies within you, train up your young children, your heirs, in the knowledge and love of godliness. Then, when they come to enjoy those fair estates they receive from you, they may become eminent for the honor of God and for the good of the country in their generation. Therefore, seek grace for yourselves and for your posterity.

3. *Based upon what we have heard, there should be moderation in all our desires for the things in this world.* Those of you who are poor should not be quite so troubled for your lack of abundance, for you see that there is a great deal of difficulty in learning how to abound. And when we are tempted to set our spirits upon the things of this world, let us curb our desires by thinking, "I see there is a great deal of difficulty in knowing how to use things; therefore let me be more moderate in my desires to gain an abundance."

Do not be overly worried about the possibility of becoming poor, and do not be so impatient and impetuous in your desire for riches. Do not envy those who are above you. Observe the risks there are of misbehavior and spiritual failure when one enjoys abundance. It may well be that God saw that you did not know how to abound, and therefore He has in mercy denied to you that which He has in wrath given to others. Remind yourselves of the example of those who have failed in their fullness, and that will be a tremendous help to you. Pray, "This man and that man have fallen due to their abundance; Lord, help me, so that I may not go astray as they have done. Yes, even Thy most eminent servants have failed; Lord, help me, that I may not do so." Then let your heart be quiet and submit to God in the condition in which He has set you.

4. *Any of you with rich friends now see the great need there is for you to pray for them.* There is a story about a godly man who once saw an acquaintance whom he had not seen for a long time and discovered that his acquaintance had become quite wealthy. Upon discovering this, he said to his friend, "Oh, sir, I had never need to pray for you so much as I do now." His friend stood amazed at this, supposing that he had heard of some great evil that had befallen him. He replied, "I hear you have had a great estate bequeathed to you." Certainly there are no men in the world who have so much need of prayer as those who are elevated by wealth.

5. *In all your abundance, learn thoroughly your utter dependence upon God.* Learn to see your need of Him as much in the midst of your abundance as in the greatest depth of affliction. That is one thing that is very useful. When a man knows that he needs just as much mercy from God in his abundance as he does in his lowest affliction, he has attained to a good measure of grace. Many men and women think they have need of God in their affliction; during such times they depend greatly

upon God. Yes, but you should depend upon God just as much if you owned the whole world as you would if you were the poorest beggar in the world.

This principle could have just as easily been placed into the category of the mystery in knowing how to abound. After all, it is indeed a mystery to the men of the world. Therefore, Christ teaches not only poor people to come and say, "Lord, give us this day our daily bread," but the richest men in the world are to pray likewise. The greatest prince or monarch in the world is to come every day to God, to the gates of mercy, and beg for his bread. Now, if rich men would be so sensible of their condition that they depend on God for the enjoyment of what they have every moment and that they need mercy just as much as the poorest man on earth, this would help them greatly in learning how to abound.

I beseech you to examine whether this is the case with you. When you were poor and afflicted, you acknowledged that you needed mercy. Yes, but do you find that now, in your abundance, you live your life as dependently on God as you ever did? If God would take away all you have, then you would think, "Oh, I must live completely the life of dependence!" But certainly you should live the life of dependence now, as if you didn't know from where you would get your next lunch or dinner. "Man lives not by bread alone," say the Scriptures, "but by every word that proceeds out of the mouth of God." He lives by it. There is a lot to be said about this, but I will give you only a few further admonitions to help you learn this lesson of knowing how to abound.

Just consider how merciful God has been to you in this! The great work before you now is to learn how to best use the riches God has mercifully given you; the work of other men is to learn how to get such riches. With other men, their only cares and thoughts are how they can get the necessities; that which God calls you to is to make better use of what you already have. The life of many men and women is nothing more than learning how to better use their wealth—not to bear much affliction or seek to gain more than they have—rather, the whole course of their life is to be spent in improving their use of the riches that they have received.

Thinking only of this one thing will make you thankful: When you are with your families, think, "What do I have to do in the morning when I arise? Nothing, except to make the best use of those things that God has mercifully given me. I am confronted with God's mercy toward me in the morning when I arise; mercy goes out into the world with me, and mercy comes back in again with me. I have nothing to do from the beginning of the year to the end of the year but to make good use of His mercies." Why, this is the life of many: to receive mercies from God and to make use of them for Him. Oh, the comfortable life that you have!

Therefore, seeing that God has placed upon you such a notable and excellent task, you need to be faithful. Your work is a great deal better and more comfortable than the work of others; therefore, examine your heart often. Oh, how I wish that I could just prevail this far with men and women who have great fortunes: that they would never let a day pass without calling themselves to self-examination! Examine yourself by saying, "Have I learned to be full? Do I enjoy my fullness for God—yes or no?" And do not let these reckonings between God and your soul lapse for too long; keep your books even every day with God. Then you shall not only have an abundance of fullness, but an abundance of comfort as well.

6. *While you may be above others in your abundance, let your hearts be attentive to the meager, low condition of others.* Be aware of their straits and their burdens, and let it be your honor to relieve their burdens. Second Corinthians 8:7 says, "Therefore, as ye abound in every thing… see that ye abound in this grace also" (this refers to the grace of liberality). In 2 Samuel 24:23, it is said of Araunah that he gave like a king. Some of you have gloried in the fact that you have spent like kings; instead, let it be your glory that you give like kings.

7. *To those whom God has given these mercies, I say this in closing: praise Him for His blessings, but especially praise Him if He has blessed His blessings to you.* Learn to thank Him when these blessings point you to Him. When we receive a blessing, we should praise God; yes,

but when God has blessed this blessing, then our praising of Him should be double—and triple too. Oh, think this way with yourself: "What? All this and heaven too? My residence is surrounded with conveniences, but I am also surrounded with mercy wherever I am! All this and heaven, house and estate, friends, health of body, and everything I want. Oh, the greatest thing that I need is a thankful heart, for if I had but that, then I would be happy indeed."

Now, if a man has all things amply supplied to him and yet is meager in his thankfulness, that means he is full in every way except for his empty heart. The heart of a wicked person is worth little. Your house is full, as is your estate, but what has become of your heart in the meantime? But if God gives you so much mercy in the world and you consider all of this to be just the beginning of heaven to you, then oh, how sweet has God made your life! And all things that are the means of the undoing of others are the means to help you honor God. Oh, by this the mercies of God are elevated indeed. Praise God for so great a blessing! It is not an ordinary thing.

CHAPTER 10

Concluding Words on Contentment

Allow me to wrap all this up by saying just one more thing related to my text. It concerns the joining of both these things together—that is, learning contentment in times of want as well as in times of plenty. The final thing I would like to add is this: grace will help men to carry themselves evenly and graciously with God in a variety of conditions. Let the condition be up or down, this way and then another way—grace helps a man to react consistently in any condition. Like dice, you may cast them whichever way you will, yet they will still land evenly. So put a gracious heart into any condition, full or empty, and grace will help him lie evenly whatever his condition. The apostle Paul said in 2 Corinthians 6:7–8, "By the armor of righteousness on the right hand and on the left, by honour and dishonour, by evil report and good report." We find use for our weapons on the right hand and on the left. The armor of righteousness helps not only on the left hand, to fence off the evil of adversity, but on the right hand, to fence off the evil of prosperity. A true Christian soldier is one who can make use of the armor of righteousness both on the right hand and on the left. Allow me to give you some reasons grace will help in any condition.

The wheels of a good watch will stay in constant and steady motion, even if a man sits on it or if it is dropped or thrown around. So it is with the heart of a man: if there is grace within and the wheels work rightly, grace will keep the heart steadfast. Let the conditions be as various as possible, whether tossed up or down, this way or that way; the heart will stay the same. Queen Elizabeth's motto ought to be the motto of every grace-filled heart: "Always be the same." So in a constant way, whether in prosperity or adversity, the gracious man will still respond consistently before God. If God brings illness upon him, he rejoices in God and blesses Him; you will find pleasant and spiritual things coming from him even then. And if God delivers him and he comes into prosperity, there you will find that his heart still remains heavenly. It remains gracious, spiritual, and raised above created things, no matter which condition he is put into. I will not give the reasons for this; I'll compare only a Scripture or two together in conclusion to demonstrate this point.

There is an evenness of the heart to be found in a godly man in all conditions, let them be what they will. In Psalm 57, we read, "To the chief Musician, Al-Taschith, Michtam of David, when he fled from Saul in the cave."

That is the title of the psalm. In other words, "A psalm that David made in his very great affliction, when he fled from Saul for his life in the cave."

Now compare that with Psalm 60, which says, "To the chief Musician upon Shushan-eduth, Michtam of David, to teach; when he strove with Aram-naharaim, and with Aram-zobah, when Joab returned, and smote of Edom in the valley of salt twelve thousand." David was in a low condition when he fled from Saul in the cave. At that time, David did not have the kingdom; afterward, however, David was exalted and had the kingdom. At that time Joab, his officer, struck down twelve thousand Edomites in the Valley of Salt.

Now, you would think that David's different conditions would have worked very differently on his spirit, yet you shall find David's heart in Psalms 57 and 60 to be very much the same. In Psalm 57:7–9 he says, "My heart is fixed, O God, my heart is fixed: I will sing and give praise. Awake up, my glory; awake, psaltery and harp: I myself will awake early. I will praise thee, O Lord, among the people: I will sing unto thee among the nations." Likewise you shall find David in Psalm 60 praising God. He praises God just as well in the prosperous state which he was in, as he does in his afflicted state.

Now compare Psalm 57:5 with Psalm 108:5; both say, "Be thou exalted, O God." David uses the same expression in his prosperity in Psalm 108 that he uses in his affliction in Psalm 57. Consider the first three verses of Psalm 108: "O God, my heart is fixed; I will sing and give praise, even with my glory. Awake, psaltery and harp: I myself will awake early. I will praise thee, O LORD, among the people: and I will sing praises unto thee among the nations." He repeats the very same words used in Psalm 57.

But now further compare Psalm 60 with Psalm 108. In Psalm 60, he says, "God hath spoken in his holiness: I will rejoice, I will divide Shechem, and mete out the valley of Succoth. Gilead is mine…Ephraim also is the strength of mine head; Judah is my lawgiver" (vv. 6–7). And in Psalm 108 he says, "God hath spoken in his holiness: I will rejoice, I will divide Shechem" (v. 7). In Psalm 108 David repeats words from times of affliction (Psalm 57) and from times of prosperity (Psalm 60).

So, although David was in these various conditions, sometimes more prosperous than others, you still find him to have the same spirit and using almost the very same words. Whether he was in the cave or when Joab had overcome or afterward, when he was in a higher condition (for Psalm 108 was written during some time after this), yet David's heart is the same—praising God, blessing God, believing in His Word, and trusting in His Word.

To apply this to yourself, you should consider whether you can make use of the same Scripture in one condition as well as in another. Are you able to make use of those Scriptures which comfort you in one condition in another condition? Consider whether you can praise God in one condition just as well as you can in another condition. God's grace so satisfies and strengthens the heart that the things that are outside of it in the world make very little difference to it. External things cannot alter a heart full of grace. When a man or woman is the sort of person who is puffed up by a prosperous condition or dejected by adversity, it is a sign of very little grace in their hearts—or perhaps of no grace at all.

It is a great part of the glory of God to be unchangeable and yet to operate in the midst of changeable circumstances. Likewise, it is a mark of the excellence of God's image in the hearts of His saints that in a variety of conditions they too would remain the same, to know how to be abased and how to abound.

So then, you who abound, be exhorted to heed what you have heard and set yourselves upon this work of learning how to abound.

Some other
Puritan Resources

from
**REFORMATION
HERITAGE BOOKS**

A Life of Gospel Peace:
A Biography of Jeremiah Burroughs
Phillip L. Simpson

978-1-60178-122-2   Hardback, 336 pages

The writings of Jeremiah Burroughs are some of the most readable and engaging Puritan works available. Like his Puritan colleagues, Burroughs sought to explain biblical teaching in a heart-searching manner. In this biography, Phillip L. Simpson opens a window into the life and times of Burroughs, providing the context for his memorable sermons and writings. What becomes apparent is Burroughs's consistent application of the principles he preached to the conduct of his life. An ardent call for a gospel-driven life and a peaceable character is reflected in both his books and life, which stand out remarkably in an era of turmoil and revolution. This is the first book-length biography of Jeremiah Burroughs.

"A man whose books are known and treasured almost four centuries after his death is a man worth getting to know. Phillip Simpson has done the church a great service in penning this long-overdue account of the life and impact of Jeremiah Burroughs. I am glad to commend it to you."

— Tim Challies, editor of *DiscerningReader.com*

Moses' Self-Denial

Jeremiah Burroughs

978-1-60178-094-2   Hardback, 160 pages

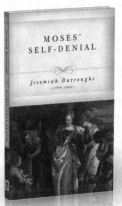

Reflecting on Hebrews 11:24–25, Jeremiah Burroughs ponders how Moses relinquished his noble and comfortable rights as the son of Pharaoh's daughter to find greater honor as a suffering son of Abraham. Burroughs explains how Christians are called to deny all honors, privileges, and delights for the sake of Christ. He also shows how God is especially honored when we forgo selfish desires at a time when they seem most advantageous to us. You will benefit greatly to see how faith acts to transform losses caused by self-denial into true honor. This is an insightful, practical book—a helpful antidote for our natural selfishness.

"Jeremiah Burroughs has served us well through this book by providing a needed corrective for a church tempted to value pleasures, honors, and wealth more than Christ. I am pleased to heartily recommend this book, praying that it will challenge your soul as it has mine."

— Phillip L. Simpson, author of
*A Life of Gospel Peace: A Biography
of Jeremiah Burroughs*

Meet the Puritans

Joel R. Beeke and Randall J. Pederson

978-1-60178-000-3   Hardback, 935 pages

Meet the Puritans provides a biographical and theological introduction to the Puritans whose works have been reprinted in the last fifty years, and also gives helpful summaries and insightful analyses of those reprinted works. It contains nearly 150 biographical entries, and nearly 700 summaries of reprinted works. A very useful resource for getting into the Puritans.

"As furnaces burn with ancient coal and not with the leaves that fall from today's trees, so my heart is kindled with the fiery substance I find in the old Scripture-steeped sermons of Puritan pastors. A warm thanks to the authors of *Meet the Puritans* for all the labor to make them known."

— John Piper, Pastor,
Bethlehem Baptist Church,
Minneapolis, Minnesota